## On Assignment With
# NATIONAL
# GEOGRAPHIC

ON ASSIGNMENT WITH

# NATIONAL GEOGRAPHIC

## THE INSIDE STORY OF LEGENDARY EXPLORERS, PHOTOGRAPHERS, AND ADVENTURERS

WRITTEN BY
MARK COLLINS JENKINS

NATIONAL GEOGRAPHIC

WASHINGTON, D.C

◀ 1997 Suspended above Antarctica's breathtaking Queen Maud Land, Conrad Anker scales a previously unclimbed peak nicknamed "the razor" using a rope-ascending device. The landscape looked "so alien we felt as if we should be wearing space suits," said Jon Krakauer of the 1997 expedition.

# CONTENTS

◀ **1947** Told to "do India," photographer Kurt Wentzel spent nearly two years traveling
the subcontinent and logged over 40,000 miles in his rehabbed WWII ambulance.
The truck served as a mobile hotel, darkroom, and billboard advertising his adventure.

# INTRODUCTION

## MISSION FORWARD

Like the song says, it's been a "long, strange trip" indeed—long as in 125 action-packed years, and strange in that this has been such an extraordinary voyage. Many an exotic shore heaves into view, of course, when your beat is "the world and all that is in it," to quote our second President, Alexander Graham Bell, but the unfamiliar, the unexplored, the unknown has always spelled opportunity for National Geographic. We have always asked who, where, why, how, and increasingly what if. It is part of our heritage. It's who we are.

The story of how we got that way is rooted in the late 19th century. In January 1888, 33 of the most prominent scientific men in the United States met in Washington, D.C., to form a society for "the increase and diffusion of geographical knowledge," as they described their mission in the organization's charter. Among them was Henry Gannett, a leading cartographer who is often called the father of American mapmaking; and John Russell Bartlett, commander of the research vessel Blake and the oceanographer after whom the Bartlett Deep (the deepest area of the Caribbean Sea) is named. Another was John Wesley Powell, who was not only an influential geologist and the Grand Canyon's most famous explorer but was also a pioneering conservationist. All of them were passionate, energetic men who believed in the power of science to effect change for the better—and who furthermore hoped to interest the general public in their work. So they inaugurated a lecture program and began publishing a quarterly journal.

▼ **2012** James Cameron emerges from *DEEPSEA CHALLENGER*, having completed the first solo dive to the ocean's deepest spot, the Mariana Trench.

The extraordinary part is how that journal was transformed into the world-famous *National Geographic* magazine, and how that small group of explorers became the booming international institution the Society is today, familiar to hundreds of millions of people around the globe. The Society has now awarded more than 10,000 scientific research grants in fields ranging from anthropology to zoology, and has seen a multitude of new discoveries and achievements, from new dinosaur fossils to the charting of the stars.

That is the big story told in this small book—the story of our Society's first 125 years. It is a tale rich in adventure and exploration and spiced with a cast of unforgettable characters. As we embark on our second century and a quarter, National Geographic is resonating with excitement and energy, pulsing with new ideas for meeting new challenges. We're just getting started.

—RENEE BRADEN
Director, National Geographic Archives

# An Invitation to Explore

*"The members of our Society will not be confined to professional geographers, but will include that large number who, like myself, desire to promote special researches by others, and to diffuse the knowledge… so that we may all know more of the world upon which we live."*

**GARDINER GREENE HUBBARD**

◀ **1896** Flouting prudish conventions of the day, *National Geographic* dared to publish photos of cultures "as they are." This portrait of a Zulu bride and groom on their wedding day was published in the November issue.

▲ **1888** Prompted by a desire to share their scientific interests, ideas, and findings, the 33 founders of the National Geographic Society first met at the Cosmos Club in Washington, D.C., on January 13, 1888. This 1963 painting depicts discussions leading up to the momentous decision to establish an organization dedicated to "the increase and diffusion of geographical knowledge." The round table is still used in the Society's headquarters today.

From the top of Mount Everest to the depths of the sea, from the world beneath the microscope to the stars in distant galaxies, the National Geographic Society has reported on "the world and all that is in it" for over a century. More than eight million members and an ever increasing global audience turn to the National Geographic Society's magazines, books, television channel, educational products, and website to increase their understanding of earth, sea, and sky and to spark their sense of wonder.

The seed for this global audience was planted in Washington, D.C., on January 13, 1888. A group of 33 of the city's scientific and intellectual leaders met at the Cosmos Club on that chilly night to consider "the advisability of organizing a society for the increase and diffusion of geographical knowledge."

They were energetic men with widely ranging professions as geologists, geographers, meteorologists, cartographers, bankers, lawyers, naturalists, soldiers, and sailors. What they had in common was the desire to promote scientific study and make the results available to the public. Many were in their 20s and 30s and actively pursuing careers that took them to places far removed from the smoky, high-ceilinged Cosmos Club. They wandered far and wide in the pursuit of science, but each autumn they returned to Washington from fieldwork posts in the deserts of the West, the forests of Alaska, or far out on the oceans. Washington, D.C., was home to most of the federal government's leading scientific bureaus: the U.S. Geological Survey, the Coast and Geodetic Survey, the

Navy Hydrographic Office, and the Smithsonian Institution, to name a few. In such places they analyzed their data, wrote up their results, and sought funding for another season in the field. They helped transform wintertime Washington into a vibrant city of intellectual activity.

▲ **1888** Gardiner Greene Hubbard (above), the Society's first President, signed the original invitation to the Cosmos Club (below).

The founders certainly embodied the spirit of adventure and discovery that has come to be associated with the National Geographic Society. Among their ranks was John Wesley Powell, famous for his pioneering exploration of the Grand Canyon, and Adolphus W. Greely, chief signal officer of the U.S. Army and a noted polar explorer who in 1881 had led an expedition to Canada's Lady Franklin Bay. Though one of his men achieved a new "farthest north" mark, Greely's expedition ended tragically—just 5 of 25 men survived being marooned for three years without being resupplied, and Greely himself was rescued within hours of certain

WASHINGTON, D. C., *January 10, 1888.*

DEAR SIR:

You are invited to be present at a meeting to be held in the Assembly Hall of the Cosmos Club, on Friday evening, January 13, at 8 o'clock P. M., for the purpose of considering the advisability of organizing a society for the increase and diffusion of geographical knowledge.

Very respectfully, yours,

GARDINER G. HUBBARD.

A. W. GREELY,
*Chief Signal Officer, U. S. A.*

J. R. BARTLETT,
*Commander, U. S N.*

HENRY MITCHELL,
*U. S. Coast and Geod. Survey.*

HENRY GANNETT,
*U. S. Geol. Survey.*

A. H. THOMPSON,
*U. S. Geol. Survey*

AND OTHERS.

▲ **1877** Founder Clarence Dutton surveyed the Grand Canyon region (above); Adolphus Greely (below) explored the Arctic.

death. Grove Karl Gilbert, the nation's leading geologist, was also at the Cosmos Club meeting, as was Henry Gannett, a distinguished cartographer. George Kennan, a former telegraph operator and Russian explorer, had spent years living in Siberia and wrote a book about the experience. Kennan was the lone representative of a profession, journalism, that likely most of the others thought would be of little relevance in the new organization's future.

Two weeks after the first meeting at the Cosmos Club, the founders elected lawyer and financier Gardiner Greene Hubbard the first President of the fledgling Society. Although not a scientist himself, Hubbard had a keen interest in science and was a staunch supporter of scientific research; most notably, he financed and promoted the experiments of his son-in-law, Alexander Graham Bell, a teacher of the deaf who had invented the telephone in 1875.

In his introductory speech, Hubbard emphasized his lack of scientific training, declaring, "by my election, you notify the public that the members of our Society will not be confined to professional geographers, but will include that large number who, like myself, desire to promote special researches by others, and to diffuse the knowledge so gained, among men, so that we may all know more of the world upon which we live."

As the new Society set these lofty goals, the United States was about to enter a great era of innovation and discovery. In 1888 Thomas Edison invented the kinetoscope, a prototype for motion pictures, and George Eastman perfected the box camera and black-and-white roll film. Automobiles and airplanes would soon become new means of transportation, and telegraphs and telephones were beginning to change the way people communicated.

Though much of the world remained to be explored, scientists were amassing knowledge on a tremendous scale. An enormous amount of energy and optimism was afoot, as was the passionate belief that science had the power to correct many of the social and economic defects of a society entering the modern era.

The new National Geographic Society would be a force in this scientific evangelism. Many scientific associations of the period shared this vision. What would set the National Geographic Society apart would be its century-long appeal to the explorer in all of us. That has allowed it to become what it is today: one of the largest scientific and educational associations on the globe, providing a window on the wonders of the world and influencing the lives of millions. ■

▲ **1881** Adolphus Greely's battered diary bears witness to his Arctic hardships.

▼ **1885** George Kennan's writings on Russia exposed the cruelties of the tsar's regime.

# THE WORLD AND ALL THAT IS IN IT

*"The world and all that is in it is our theme, and if we can't find anything to interest ordinary people in that we better shut up shop."*

ALEXANDER GRAHAM BELL

◀ **1909** Portrait of explorer Robert E. Peary as a cold man

CIRCA 1900 Whenever the cherry trees flowered in Japan, Eliza Scidmore set up her camera, for the trembling blossoms "filled the people with joy."

**▲ 1873** One-armed Civil War veteran, geologist, explorer, and Society founder John Wesley Powell speaks with a Paiute Indian. At age 35 Powell led the first expedition by boat down the Colorado River through the Grand Canyon.

T he first issue of *National Geographic*, published in October 1888, was a modest-looking scientific brochure with an austere terra-cotta cover. The featured article was a dense, scholarly report by WJ McGee on "The Classification of Geographic Forms by Genesis." Yet also tucked into the issue was an account of the Great Storm of March 11–14, which opened with isotherms and meteorological charts but ended in a riveting description of the survival of the New York–based pilot boat *Charles H. Marshall*. From the start the magazine presented an interesting mix of science and adventure.

While it had neither a paid staff nor an official head-quarters, the Society lobbied to establish the U.S. Board

**◄ 1888** The first issue of *National Geographic* magazine appeared in October and was sent to the Society's nearly 200 members. It contained mostly reprints of papers that had been presented at recent meetings.

on Geographic Names, which in 1890 began untangling the confusion of place-names scattered over the map of the continent. The Society also began presenting gold medals for outstanding student essays on geography. And at the 1893 Chicago World's Fair, National Geographic sponsored the first international meeting of geographers ever held in America.

In the era before television and movies, when travel was still a luxury reserved for the well-to-do, the National Geographic Society delivered a world of adventure to its Washington members by inviting prominent explorers and scientists to speak about their work. In February 1888, just one month after the Society's founding, explorer John Wesley Powell inaugurated the lecture series by delivering a talk about the physical geography of the United States.

Very quickly the Society began attracting explorers eager to tell their stories, including Fridtjof Nansen, an Arctic explorer; Gifford Pinchot, founder of the U.S. Forest Service; and mountaineer Annie S. Peck, who told of climbing peaks in the Alps and volcanoes in Mexico. Thousands gathered to hear Roald Amundsen, soon to be the first man to reach the South Pole, discuss his pioneering navigation of the Northwest Passage. Women constituted a large number of lecture attendees. They found the lectures enlightening as well as entertaining.

In 1889 National Geographic published its first color illustrations—pastel drawings of scenes from Nicaragua—as well as the first authoritative four-color foldout map, which would soon become an important part of the magazine. And in the spring

▲ **1891** Society lectures quickly became popular Washington events. Above, a ticket from Robert Peary's lecture on his Greenland expedition. Proceeds from his lectures helped Peary fund his expeditions to the Arctic.

▲ **1913** Polar explorers and other Society luminaries gathered at the Society to present Roald Amundsen with a medal for being the first to reach the South Pole.

▲ **1890** Gripping their alpenstocks, members of the Society's first expedition begin exploring Alaska's Mount St. Elias. William Lindsley's journal (below) records their harrowing attempts to summit the mountain.

of 1890 the two-year-old Society sponsored its first expedition into the field, teaming with the U.S. Geological Survey.

Ten men, led by geologist Israel C. Russell, explored and surveyed Mount St. Elias, the highest point on the boundary between Alaska and Canada. The expedition set the pattern for the Society's expeditions to come, as well as the tone of the magazine's first-person adventure-narrative accounts. "Darkness settled and rain fell in torrents," Russell wrote, "beating through our little tent. We rolled ourselves in blankets, determined to rest in spite of the storm. Avalanches, already numerous, became more frequent. A crash told of tons of ice and rock sliding down on the glacier."

Membership in these early years was largely confined to men in the scientific circles of Washington and their families and friends. A volunteer committee edited the magazine, which faithfully listed the names of the Society's several hundred members in each issue, reported the minutes of their meetings, and documented group picnics and field trips to nearby Civil War battlefields. It also ran a number of articles that, as one journalist later observed, "were suitable for diffusing geographic knowledge among those who already had it and scaring off the rest."

The magazine, published only sporadically, floundered commercially, and in 1896 the Board of Managers, hoping to boost circulation, placed the *Geographic* on newsstands, began to solicit advertising, and made the 25-cent journal into an "Illustrated Monthly" in imitation of the day's more successful magazines, *Harper's Weekly* and *Munsey's*. John Hyde, a statistician with the Department of Agriculture, became Editor and began to insert an occasional photograph, a practice some prominent members considered frivolous.

Despite such grumblings, in 1896 Hyde published a startling photograph unlike any other then printed by an American magazine. It was a wedding photo—a half-nude Zulu bride and groom in a gentle pose. This bold move—to show cultures as they really were—would become characteristic of the magazine.

In 1897 Gardiner Greene Hubbard died and his son-in-law Alexander Graham Bell was elected to the office of President. Inventor of the telephone, pioneer of flight, teacher of the deaf, he was nearly 51 years old and fully immersed in a number of scientific projects. He was reluctant to take the job. But the organization was on the brink of bankruptcy. Bell agreed to lead the Society, as he later wrote in his journal, only "in order to save it."

Bell had a number of ideas. He told the governing board he wanted members of a Society rather than readers of a magazine. Do not depend on fickle newsstand sales; subscriptions to *National Geographic* should come only with membership, he

▼ **1912** Proud to support science and exploration, people often displayed membership certificates in their homes.

▼ **1890** Although a photograph of a map had appeared in the third issue of the magazine, this modest image of Russia's Herald Island published in July was the first photograph of a natural scene.

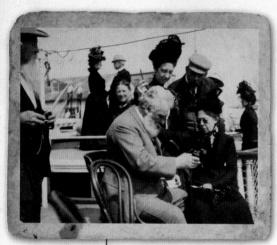

▲ **1900** Society President Alexander Graham Bell prepares to view a total eclipse of the sun during a National Geographic excursion to Norfolk, Virginia, on May 28. Most of the Society's few hundred members participated in the trip.

said. Shrewdly, Bell emphasized the founders' wishes: Not just the scientific elite, but schoolteachers, nurses, construction workers, and salesmen might be interested in funding expeditions to Peru and dispatching explorers to the South Pole.

Bell further insisted that these new members should actually be able to read and enjoy the articles. He wanted no more obtuse and undecipherable academic tracts. And, what's more, he insisted on "pictures, and plenty of them."

To help implement his new ideas Bell cast about for a full-time Editor who could relieve the overtaxed John Hyde. He found Gilbert Hovey Grosvenor, 23 years old, an instructor at a boys' academy in New Jersey. Not only a challenge but also a romance lured young "Bert" Grosvenor to Washington in 1899. His father, noted historian Edwin A. Grosvenor, had lectured at the Society a few years earlier and had visited the Bells. Talk turned to the professor's twin sons, Gilbert and Edwin, who would graduate from Amherst in the spring. The Bells' eligible daughters, Elsie and Daisy, were listening closely. When the Grosvenors later invited the Bell sisters to attend the Amherst graduation, they accepted with pleasure, and

▶ **1920s** Amherst graduate Gilbert H. Grosvenor, pictured here at his desk, began working at the National Geographic Society on April 1, 1899. He would remain at his post for another 55 years.

Elsie was intrigued by the courtly Gilbert. It was she who dropped the young man's name in her father's ear that spring as Bell was looking for his new Editor.

When Gilbert Grosvenor arrived in Washington for an interview, Bell pushed copies of the nation's best magazines—McClure's, Munsey's, Harper's Weekly—in front of him and asked, "Can you create a geographic magazine as popular as these, one that will support the Society instead of the Society being burdened with the magazine?"

Grosvenor answered yes. Elsie had only a moment with him at the door: "I told Papa you had the talent he sought," she whispered, "and would like to come to Washington." We may never know which seemed more intimidating to him, the job or the girl.

Bell hired Grosvenor as the magazine's assistant editor, at the salary of $100 a month paid out of Bell's pocket, and on April 1, 1899, took him to the rented quarters where the Geographic shared an office with the American Forestry Society. Grosvenor found that the entire inventory of the National Geographic Society comprised "two rickety chairs, a small table, a litter of papers and ledgers, and six enormous boxes crammed with Geographics returned by the newsstands."

Gilbert Grosvenor was the Society's first full-time employee, and the job he had just undertaken would consume his energy for a lifetime. To boost membership, he sent letters to prominent Washington men to "nominate their friends" for election to membership, making sure the letters were on expensive, embossed paper. The flattery recruited many, and membership took an upturn.

Under Grosvenor National Geographic magazine covered a world of topics ranging from "Korea: the Hermit Nation" to British shipbuilding to Robert E. Peary's latest Arctic expedition to measuring the height of Mount Rainier. He took as

▲ **1900s** A strong and often vocal supporter of women's right to vote, Elsie May Bell Grosvenor (above) was involved in many Society activities and designed the first Society flag in 1903. Its bands of brown, green, and blue (below) represent earth, sea, and sky.

## ELIZA SCIDMORE

**B**orn in the U.S. Midwest, journalist Eliza Scidmore (1856–1928) spent her life writing about what used to be called the "Far East." A great traveler, she was an influential figure in the early days of the National Geographic Society, serving as its foreign secretary, honorary associate editor, and in 1892 becoming the first woman elected to its board. A vivid writer, Scidmore authored many books on China, Java, and Japan that opened American eyes to the exotic world of Asia while also promoting a better understanding of its different peoples. Her photographs, including this hand-tinted depiction of a Japanese rice farmer (below), frequently graced the pages of *National Geographic* magazine. Above all places, she loved Japan and was personally decorated by the emperor.

his editorial cue a directive he once received from Bell:

"THE WORLD AND ALL THAT IS IN IT is our theme, and if we can't find anything to interest ordinary people in that subject we better shut up shop and become a strict, technical, scientific journal for high class geographers and geological experts."

Bell preferred popular, readable coverage on geographic topics. When news of the 1902 eruption of Mount Pelée on Martinique reached Washington, Grosvenor telegraphed Bell, who was vacationing in Nova Scotia, and sought approval to send a small scientific team to the island to investigate the eruption. Bell declined, telling the young Editor, "Go yourself to Martinique in the interests of the Magazine and I will pay your expenses . . . this is the opportunity of a lifetime— seize it. Start within 24 hours and let the world hear from you as our representative. Leave science to others and give us details of living interest beautifully illustrated by photographs."

Although Grosvenor did not go—a Society-sponsored expedition did—the point was made: *National Geographic* magazine should combine vivid storytelling with striking photographs.

Grosvenor constantly monitored public opinion and looked for ways to boost interest in the magazine. He used the Society's popular lecture series as a barometer to gauge interest in sub-

jects and illustrations. Arcane addresses on topography or land use drew an average of 20 attendees. But on the night that a scientist who had gone to Martinique lectured on the eruption of Mount Pelée, the 1,200-seat theater was packed. Unfortunately the speaker brought no illustrations. Grosvenor overheard two young women complain: "Why doesn't he show photographs? That's what we want."

Grosvenor needed no further convincing. After all, photography was a frank, scientific way of looking at the world, although many intellectuals continued to dismiss it as superficial, if not vulgar. Undeterred, Grosvenor began energetically scouring the city for photo collections and archives. In 1903 the Society moved to its first headquarters building, Hubbard Hall, six blocks north of the White House on 16th Street. Grosvenor became both full-fledged

▲ **1900s** Father-in-law Bell and two of Grosvenor's children pay a visit to the Editor at Beinn Bhreagh, the family's summer home in Baddeck, Nova Scotia. Grosvenor often retreated from the hubbub to the solitude of this tent, where he edited articles for *National Geographic*, sending the finished manuscripts back to Washington.

▸ **1906** The art nouveau design on the cover of the December *Geographic* was the fifth cover format since 1888. In 1910 the magazine assumed its familiar oak-and-laurel leaved look, basis for the yellow border of today.

▲ **1895** Portrait of explorer Robert E. Peary as a young man

▼ **1909** Guides, sled dogs, and crew crowd the deck of Peary's ship on "a mild day."

Editor and Director of Society operations. Soon after, Alexander Graham Bell stepped down as President. Though retired, he never lost interest in the magazine, sending his son-in-law packages of story ideas and photographs while contributing articles, often on tetrahedral kites or other strange flying machines. Bell continued offering pertinent editorial advice, once noting, "The features of most importance are the illustrations ... The disappointing feature of the Magazine is that there is so little in the text about the pictures ... It seems to me that one notable line for improvement would be either to adapt the pictures to the text or the text to the pictures. Why not the latter?"

It was prescient advice. In late 1904, when the printer told him he had to quickly fill 11 pages, Grosvenor reached for a package that had just arrived from two Russian explorers. Inside were rare photographs of Lhasa, Tibet, among the most mysterious cities in the world. Picking out a dozen, he sent them to the

printer with only brief photo captions, adapting the text to the pictures. Knowing this was close to heresy for a serious magazine, he feared he might be fired. But when the January 1905 issue appeared, friends, even strangers, stopped him on the street offering congratulations.

Three months later, in the April 1905 *Geographic*, Grosvenor published a staggering 138 photographs of the Philippines obtained free from the U.S. government through his cousin, William Howard Taft, former U.S. commissioner for the Philippines and soon to be President of the United States. The issue was so popular it was soon reprinted.

▲ **1909** Peary often carried a lightweight, portable roll-film camera on his Arctic expeditions.

In July 1906 Grosvenor devoted an entire issue to wildlife: "Photographing Wild Game with Flashlight and Camera," written and shot by George Shiras 3d, a former U.S. congressman who had replaced his gun with a camera. Seventy-four candid photographs captured animals—deer, porcupines, and a lynx—as they tripped across triggers in the darkness. Shiras' photos caused a sensation. President Theodore Roosevelt was enthralled, and letters poured in from readers demanding more natural history. The impact of photos was now beyond dispute. In two years, membership had jumped from 3,000 to 20,000. The National Geographic Society had become the largest geographic organization on the globe.

▼ **1905** The January *Geographic* with a twist—a picture story—11 full pages of photos. The issue's popularity helped confirm Grosvenor's faith in the editorial value of photography.

Grosvenor never looked back. Using photography as his lens on the world, he filled the pages of the magazine with wonders: Egyptian tombs, Chinese canals, Canadian Rockies, even

# THE ENDS OF THE EARTH

## EXPLORING THE POLES

▲ **1921** Men and dogs cross treacherous ice floes in the Arctic on the MacMillan Expedition.

▼ **1926** The sun compass designed for Richard Byrd's polar flights

hat imaginary point—the aloof and lonely bottom of the earth" was how Richard E. Byrd described the South Pole. In 1888, when the National Geographic Society was founded, both North and South Poles did seem more imaginary than real, mere blanks on the world map. But the Society came of age during one of the great eras in polar exploration.

The commanding figure of Robert E. Peary was the Geographic's first polar hero. The Society showered him with grants and gold medals and championed his claim to have been first to reach the North Pole on April 6, 1909. National Geographic also welcomed to its headquarters the legendary Antarctic explorer Sir

Ernest Shackleton as well as the discoverer of the South Pole, Roald Amundsen. And in 1925, icy-eyed Donald MacMillan led a Society expedition that was the first to use airplanes and short-wave radio to explore the Arctic.

In Richard E. Byrd the Geographic found a second polar hero. In 1926 Byrd and a co-pilot may have been first to fly over the North

◄ 1957 On assignment to Antarctica, staff photographer Thomas J. Abercrombie—the first journalist to reach the South Pole—scrapes ice from his beard at the International Geophysical Year's South Pole station. That evening, the temperature dropped to -102.1°F.

Pole, a feat made possible by a navigational sun compass provided him by the Society. Three years later, in 1929, carrying both the sun compass and a National Geographic flag, Byrd and four companions became the first to fly over the South Pole as well. Byrd's large expeditions mapped many previously unknown Antarctic peaks, and Byrd named Mount Grosvenor and Mount La Gorce after Society officers.

The heroic age of polar exploration has given way to one of aircraft, icebreakers, and permanent research stations. Yet determined individuals with dogsleds still occasionally slog over the ice and into the pages of National Geographic. One is Will Steger, first to lead dogsled teams both to the North Pole and across the vast extent of Antarctica. In 1995 Steger became the Society's first explorer-in-residence. ∎

▲ 1909 The diagonal patch missing from Peary's flag was ripped off and left at the North Pole.

**▲ 1907** Thirty years after the Battle of Little Bighorn, Sioux Chief Red Hawk (above), who fought against Custer, reenacts the battle for photographer Edward Curtis. Curtis's work was featured in the July issue of *National Geographic*. His famous 20-volume work documents nearly every tribe in western North America.

backyard insects. Occasionally the articles were products of their times; there is, for instance, more than a whiff of imperialism in "French Conquest of the Sahara" and "The Non-Christian Peoples of the Philippine Islands with an account of what has been done for them under American Rule." But alongside such period pieces were ones of more enduring value. The July 1907 issue featured some of the timeless photographic portraits of Native Americans made by Edward Curtis, who spent a lifetime documenting the disappearing tribes of the American West.

Paintings occasionally supplemented photographs. "Fifty Common Birds of Farm and Orchard," published in June 1913, was originally printed as an agricultural pamphlet. Grosvenor, fast becoming a passionate bird-watcher, borrowed the color plates with their exquisite paintings of birds.

The result was an issue so popular that for many years birds were a perennial staple in the magazine.

The success of *National Geographic* meant increased support for exploration and discovery. In 1907 the Society awarded a grant to Cmdr. Robert E. Peary in support of his forthcoming attempt to reach the North Pole. Peary had already made several arduous treks north, and for these pioneering explorations the Society presented him with the first Hubbard Medal, its highest honor. Standing on feet crippled by frostbite at the Society's annual white-tie banquet, the determined Peary accepted the medal from President Theodore Roosevelt and vowed to reach his goal. For the true explorer, Peary said, "The thing he has set himself to do is a part of his very being."

▼ 1912 Two years
before the Panama Canal
opened to traffic, the
magazine published this
bird's-eye-view map.

Peary and his crew, including the skilled African-American
explorer Matthew Henson, arrived at the top of the world on
April 6, 1909. Or at least Peary claimed that they did. Frederick
A. Cook's rival boast—that he had reached the Pole a year
earlier—was dismissed for lack of evidence. Though a Society
committee concluded that Peary did get there, and nearly
every geographic body in the
world subsequently agreed,
doubts still linger.

By 1912 the Society had
grown strong enough to
record a $43,000 surplus,
which was earmarked spe-
cifically for the support
of scientific exploration.
Soon the Geographic
became one of the nation's

primary sponsors of scientific expeditions, and the magazine became the publication of record for discovery. Furthermore the Society continued to honor prominent explorers and scientists. In 1910 it bestowed its Hubbard Medal on Sir Ernest Shackleton for coming within 112 miles of the South Pole, and in 1913 it conferred a Special Gold Medal on Roald Amundsen for being first to actually arrive there.

▲ **1910** Battling the ice pack at Alaska's Disenchantment Bay, glaciologists Ralph S. Tarr and Lawrence Martin led this expedition to map and monitor fluctuations in numerous glaciers. Their research, based on three separate expeditions, was published by the Society in 1914 as *Alaskan Glacier Studies*, a book that guided glacier research for decades and helped scientists understand North America's ice ages.

One of the most exciting Society-sponsored expeditions was Hiram Bingham's search among the highlands of Peru for a legendary Inca capital. After Bingham found the astonishing abandoned Inca city of Machu Picchu, the dramatic story of his quest and discoveries filled all 186 pages of the April 1913 issue. In 1915 Robert Griggs explored Alaska's Mount Katmai Peninsula, scene three years earlier of the largest volcanic eruption of the 20th century. The Society eventually awarded grants for six expeditions to the area, part of which was fissured with spectacular steam vents. Griggs named that region the Valley of Ten Thousand Smokes, and it was later designated a national monument.

When in 1916 the Society interceded with money to help preserve an important stand of California sequoias, it had already been urging the conservation of natural resources for years. For decades to come the Society would work closely with the National Park Service, which the Society

▶ **1913** "Fifty Common Birds of Farm and Orchard" in the June *Geographic* contained fifty full-color bird portraits by Louis Agassiz Fuertes, the magazine's first showcase of the famous illustrator's work.

# EXPEDITIONS

## THE HEART OF
## NATIONAL GEOGRAPHIC

▲ **1912** The supply list for the Griggs expedition includes powdered eggs and Lumberman socks.

In 1890 Israel C. Russell led the Society's first expedition to map Mount St. Elias in Alaska. Since then the National Geographic Society has funded over 10,000 grants for research and expeditions to almost every corner of the Earth. Formalized as the Committee for Research and Exploration in 1916, the CRE gathers a board of distinguished scientists to review applications and grant funds to scientists from all over the world. After conducting fieldwork, grantees write up their findings and send reports to Society headquarters. Some of their results may be featured in *National Geographic* magazine or in National Geographic's books, on the website, or on television. Through Society sponsorship, William Beebe and Otis Barton made their pioneering half-mile ocean descent in a steel bathysphere (1934) and Jane Goodall ventured into the African forest to study chimp behavior (1961). Recently the CRE has supported Robert Ballard's Black Sea work, which has uncovered well-preserved Greek and Roman ships and traces of an ancient, cataclysmic flood. Grants have supported Paul Sereno's dinosaur excavations, as well as Jamie Seymour's studies of the venomous box jellyfish. Since 1998, explorers and adventurers have also received grants through the Expeditions Council, which has supported mountain climber Todd Skinner and biologist Mike Fay. ■

▲ **2002** Scientist Jésus Rivas, a herpetologist, grapples with an Amazonian anaconda. He typically captures them for study with his bare hands.

helped establish in 1916, and other agencies dedicated to preserving wilderness.

World War I underscored the growing national reach and importance of the *Geographic*. Readers opened their August 1914 edition of the magazine to find an up-to-date map of "The New Balkan States and Central Europe" that allowed them to follow the developments of the war. Large maps of the fighting fronts continued to be published throughout the conflict, and *National Geographic* kept members informed of the history and culture of the warring countries with articles on "The World's Debt to France," "Belgium's Plight," and "The German Nation." It featured stories on conditions at the front, including the prevalence of "cooties" (lice), as well as a special issue, praised by President Woodrow Wilson, on the flags and iconography of the world. The Society established a News Service Bureau to provide bulletins on the geographic aspects of the war for the nation's newspapers. Furthermore it supported a hospital ward near Paris for wounded soldiers and allowed Red Cross workers to roll bandages in the Society's library.

In 1920 the Board of Trustees elected Gilbert Hovey Grosvenor as both President and Editor. After two decades of struggle, the Society was financially stable, with a permanent staff and headquarters. As the nation slipped into the jazzed-up roaring '20s, Alexander Graham Bell died in 1922 at the age of 75. By then the formerly austere little scientific journal had become one of America's most trusted and eagerly anticipated magazines. ∎

**▼ 1918** Using *National Geographic* magazine as a classroom text, a military instructor teaches English to foreign-born soldiers at Camp Kearny, California.

**▲ 1917** "Flags of the World" issue, October

# BRINGING COLOR
## ᴛᴏ THE WORLD

*"Few men during their lifetime
come anywhere near exhausting
the resources dwelling within them.
There are deep wells of strength
that are never used."*

**RICHARD BYRD**

◄ **1931** A bandit chief's son and part-time tribal shaman poses for Joseph Rock's camera. A plant hunter by trade, Rock journeyed into the remote corners of southwestern China in the 1920s and '30s. His stories and photographs captured the region's rich ancient cultures and traditions, many of which have now disappeared.

**1900** This picturesque portrait of Jerusalem's Bab Khan el Zeit, or Olive Street, was purchased by Editor Gilbert Grosvenor for the magazine's collection.

▲ **1927** Circling the Society's headquarters building, a vast crowd clamors for tickets to see Charles Lindbergh receive the Hubbard Medal for his solo crossing of the Atlantic.

I n the first decades of the 20th century men and women fanned out to every corner of the globe in cars, airplanes, ships, and on bicycles. Explorers and adventurers made front-page news and were welcomed home with ticker-tape parades. Like baseball players, Robert E. Peary and Ernest Shackleton appeared on trading cards. And the star power of Charles Lindbergh and Amelia Earhart drew thunderous ovations wherever they went.

In spite of the exhilarating pace of exploration in the 1920s, 65 percent of Americans still lived in rural areas,

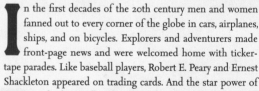

◀ **1931** Filled with thrilling stories for armchair travelers, *National Geographic* delivered the world to members' doorsteps. October 1931 featured the famous Citroën-Haardt Trans-Asiatic Expedition.

and the National Geographic provided to its members an important window on the world. As soon as new photographic processes made it possible—and well ahead of other magazines—Gilbert Grosvenor brought color to its pages. His motive was to present reality—to let readers see things as they really were. The world, after all, was in color, not black-and-white.

In 1910 National Geographic published 24 pages of photographs from Korea and Japan, shot by a wealthy, well-traveled gentleman named William Wisner Chapin. A Japanese artist hand-tinted the pictures in delicate colors. Other tinted pictures followed. Meanwhile, chemists around the world had struggled to develop real color photography. In 1907 the Lumière brothers in France devised the first practical commercial color process, using dyed grains of potato starch on a glass plate. They called it Autochrome. The first natural color photograph to appear in the magazine was an Autochrome published in the July 1914 Geographic.

But Autochromes were expensive and difficult to find. Photographers had to travel with such bulky gear and volatile chemicals that each photograph was nearly as labor-intensive as painting in oils. In 1915 the Geographic hired Franklin Fisher, who established the first color photographic laboratory in American publishing and recruited a team of artist-technicians who began to systematically show the world in photographic color for the first time. National Geographic photographers would process their Autochrome plates in the field and pack them into padded crates for steamer trips to America. Many contributing photographers never saw the headquarters in Washington throughout their distinguished careers.

▲ **1929** Navigating with a compass designed by the Society's chief cartographer Albert H. Bumstead, Richard Byrd and four companions became the first people to fly over the South Pole.

▲ **1910** The November 1910 Geographic carried 24 pages of hand-tinted images of Korea and Japan, at the time the largest collection of photographs in color ever published in a magazine.

▲ **1916** Minute grains of potato starch—dyed green, red, and blue—filtered light and captured the vivid color in this 1916 Autochrome of dancers in Indian costume.

In 1924 Fisher gained his first administrative assistant—Melville Bell Grosvenor, son of the boss, a U.S. Naval Academy graduate just released from a year of active duty with the peacetime Navy. For the next four years, Fisher and young Mel selected all of the pictures published in *National Geographic*. This was the era when even mundane assignments created photographic history. Society records glow with "firsts"—as in the "first natural color photographs of Arctic life," the "first natural color photographs from the air," and the only "natural color photographs of the coronation of Ethiopian Emperor Haile Selassie."

One "first" stands out as a true pioneering achievement. In a clear lagoon in Florida's Dry Tortugas, Charles Martin, head of the Geographic's photo lab, and ichthyologist W. H. Longley made the world's first undersea color photographs. Martin constructed a flash-powder mechanism that was synchronized to a submerged camera encased in brass. Longley carried the camera, wearing a bulky diver's helmet with air hose attached to a compressor on a dory. On the surface, Martin tended a huge reflector and enough magnesium powder to blow up the whole project. The bursts of powder were deafening and blinding, and Longley was seriously burned. Their pictures were published in January 1927.

▼ **1910** Photographer O. D. von Engeln washes his film in seawater among Alaska icebergs.

As membership soared past a million in 1926, National Geographic dispatched "photographic expeditions" to the Caribbean and South America, to western Europe and the Balkans, and to Asia. Professional writers and photographers became the explorers; accurate and penetrating documentation became the science of the expedition.

The story behind getting the story quickly became a beloved tradition among the readers of the *Geographic*. In the caption that accompanied a lively color image of folk dancers in Austria in 1938, W. Robert Moore wrote, "I took potshots standing up and lying on my stomach in the dusty courtyard. Rough boots kicked up dust, dresses, and petticoats swished; they were having an altogether good time in a spontaneous dance. So was I."

▼ **1920s–1940s**
*National Geographic* photographers carried medium- and large-format cameras like this Graflex Series B from the 1920s through the 1940s.

▲ **1926** Exploding flash powder (above) illuminates the waters around the Dry Tortugas enough to expose the first color photographs (including the hogfish at right) ever made of the undersea world. Ichthyologist W. H. Longley, who collaborated with National Geographic Society laboratory chief Charles Martin on the endeavor, was seriously burned in the process, which required igniting an entire pound of magnesium flash powder to provide enough light to brighten the sea.

Joseph Rock penetrated unknown corners of Asia, becoming the first American to visit the Kingdom of Muli in China's Sichuan Province. Rock dispatched a dozen articles to the magazine from remote Asian outposts and confided to his editor upon his return, "my soul still dwells in the great silences among the snow peaks."

In Venezuela and Brazil, Ernest G. Holt made the first systematic collections of birds and animals from previously little-known areas of South America. Ranging even farther afield, an NGS–Smithsonian–Yale University expedition to Nepal led by S. Dillon Ripley became the first Western scientific expedition to enter parts of that country in a century. It returned with a trove of specimens, including the spiny babbler, a bird long thought extinct.

In the high peaks of the Yukon, Bradford Washburn and his team embarked on a bold mapping mission by airplane, during which they mapped a 5,000-square-mile area in northern Canada that was literally a blank space before they ventured into it.

The venerable staff writer of that era, Frederick Simpich, wrote an amazing 89 stories for the *Geographic*. For decades his craggy, cheerful face made friends over most of the world. His style, too, perfectly mirrored the enthusiasm of Gilbert Grosvenor, who was never satisfied with the verb "to be." He wanted action words and dynamic prose, and Simpich tossed around exclamation marks like confetti. He was hugely popular with readers.

But no one typified the new breed more than Maynard Owen Williams, the Society's first foreign correspondent. A large, gregarious, and enthusiastic man, a former missionary in China and Syria, he contributed text or photographs, or both, to some 100 articles. Williams was present at the opening of King Tut's tomb, made color photographs of the Arctic, and was the only American selected to join the grandiose, motorized French Citroën-Haardt Expedition across Asia. Near the end of the 314-day, 7,370-mile expedition, temperatures dropped so low that Williams had to suck on his frozen fountain pen to thaw the ink. "Never grieve for me if it is my good fortune to die with my boots on," Williams once wrote to Grosvenor. "That's what I most hope for."

Williams pioneered the Foreign Editorial Staff, a legendary group of correspondents who could both write and photograph stories, often taking two years or more to cover distant parts of the world.

In the 1930s "miniature" 35-mm cameras paired with a dazzling new color film, Kodachrome, to revolutionize the magazine. Luis Marden, a self-educated,

▼ **1923** Covering the opening of Tutankhamun's tomb for the magazine, Maynard Owen Williams (below, emerging from King Tut's tomb) wrote "There is drama in the very air . . ."

▼ **1940s** The Society's headquarters as pictured in a 1940s postcard

# ON ASSIGNMENT

## THE GREATEST
## JOB IN THE WORLD?

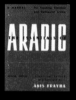

Rain. Camera malfunctions. Ruined film. Vehicle breakdowns. Uncooperative critters. Lousy guides. Customs hassles. Bureaucratic red tape. Interminable waits in train stations, in airports, in offices, for permissions, for interviews. Close encounters with unfriendly stares. Equipment stolen. Bribes demanded. Too many roaches. Too many mosquitoes. Too many mysterious maladies. Too many bouts of food poisoning. It's too hot. It's too cold. Life in the field can be a lonely and frustrating affair.

So, once again, you make do. You trudge through the rain. You improvise makeshift repairs. You engage a better guide. You smile and eat it anyway. You put up with crazy drivers, leaky boats, drunken bush pilots, stubborn mules, ill-tempered camels, even yaks, to get where you need to go. You adapt to changing circumstances—if at all possible, with aplomb and savoir faire. Your success demands resourcefulness, patience, good humor, good judgment, street smarts, and a talent for roughing it. So open your eyes, try to have fun, but always gather good material. Make the most of misadventures. If you do, and your work gives rise to a great Geographic story, then you can finally relax and admit you have the greatest

▲ **1960s** Getting along in the field requires ingenuity, good humor, and an occasional phrase of goodwill in Tahitian, Urdu, or Arabic. The dictionaries above were both used on assignment by staffers.

▶ **1940s** Filing from the field, correspondent Howell Walker (right) improvised an office in a remote

▲ **1931** Crossing Asia by pony, camel, yak, and car, Maynard Owen Williams accompanied the Citroën-Haardt expedition as chief photographer from 1931 to 1932. Though it ended abruptly with Haardt's death in 1932, Williams called the 18-month journey "the greatest adventure of my life."

multilingual color enthusiast, arrived at the Geographic in 1934 at the age of 21. He immediately saw the potential in the new combination. Kodachrome offered the richest color yet, it could be enlarged easily, and its enhanced speed—its ability to gather light—allowed photographers to shoot with small 35-mm cameras. No more tripods and posed pictures; no more glass plates packed into steamer trunks. Action pictures in color were possible for the first time. Melville Grosvenor remembered the heady intoxication: "We just threw out our other pictures from the field—just scrapped them and replaced them as fast as we could with Kodachromes. I'll never forget that—that was really a thrill."

▶ **1942** July 1942 carried the first illustration printed on the cover. At the government's request many American magazines showed the flag and encouraged people to buy savings bonds to support the war effort.

THE NATIONAL GEOGRAPHIC

AUSTRIA    K-432

W. R. MOORE

Rec'd Nov., 1937

▲ **1937** Kodachrome film freed photographers from the tyranny of posed pictures. This frame by W. Robert Moore captures the whirling action of Burgenland dancers in Austria.

By the 1930s the Society had outgrown Hubbard Hall, its original headquarters, and had built a dignified, three-story extension with wood paneling and Italian marble stairs and luxurious fittings. In 1943 the New Yorker published a three-part profile of Gilbert Grosvenor that offers a glimpse of what it was like to work at the Society in those days:

*The twenty or so editors of the Geographic, all of them notably polite individuals who are forever bowing to one another through the sculptured bronze doors of the elevators, move in a leisurely welter of thick rugs, bookshelves stocked with encyclopedias, bound volumes of the Geographic; interoffice memorandum slips with "Memorandum from Dr. Grosvenor"; incoming correspondence stamped with "Commendation," "Criticism," or "Suggestions." For business errands around town the editors have a fleet of*

▶ **1928** Sails set for the far horizon, one of Columbus's three caravels faces a new world in this painting, one of five scenes of exploration and discovery commissioned by the Society from artist N. C. Wyeth in 1926. Today the paintings hang in historic Hubbard Hall.

five chauffeur-driven cars. They lunch in three private dining rooms, drinking buttermilk, exchanging puns, and ordering excellent à la carte meals from menus on which prices are discreetly omitted.

In reality, the staff was considerably more rough around the edges. But Grosvenor's courtly manner gave the offices of the Geographic an air of refinement.

▲ **1944** During World War II National Geographic maps were widely used by the military.

When World War II came, the Geographic opened its vast files of photographs, more than 300,000 at that time, to the armed forces. By matching prewar aerial photographs against wartime ones, analysts detected camouflage and gathered intelligence. One high-ranking general wrote to Gilbert Grosvenor in 1946 that the Geographic files "proved to be the richest and most helpful single source of pictorial material" that the armed forces had.

With the wartime boost, photographic technology was exploding. Harold E. "Doc" Edgerton, a professor at Massachusetts Institute of Technology, had developed the high-speed electronic flash in 1931 and perfected it with the help of National Geographic grants. From the late 1940s through the 1970s, Edgerton was a contributor to the magazine with such mind-boggling images as a bullet frozen in the act of bursting through an apple.

▲ **1944** General Eisenhower uses a National Geographic map of Germany. Red Cross workers used Society maps to locate Japanese POW camps, and Army engineers posted the Germany map at many European intersections.

National Geographic sponsored more than 100 expeditions from the 1920s through the 1950s. Exploration in these decades sought to probe the planet's physical extremes—from Pole to Pole, from the tallest peaks to the deepest ocean trenches. The June 1931 National Geographic published William Beebe's account of climbing with Otis Barton into a steel bathysphere off Bermuda and plunging—deeper than any person before them—to depths of inky darkness. Tethered to a barge on the surface, the capsule bounced

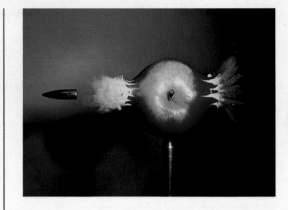

like a yo-yo as it drifted past transparent fish and pale shrimps, "ghostly things in every direction," wrote Beebe. In 1934, under Geographic sponsorship, Beebe and Barton descended nearly twice as deep, to 3,028 feet, a depth record that stood for the next 15 years.

The March 1933 *Geographic* carried the accounts of balloonist Auguste Piccard's record-breaking ascents to altitudes higher than 53,000 feet, more than 10 miles, in hydrogen-filled balloons. "The stratosphere is the superhighway of future intercontinental transport," Piccard predicted. A year later National Geographic joined the U.S. Army Air Corps to sponsor the Explorer I stratospheric balloon flight. Albert W. Stevens, William Kepner, and Orvil Anderson climbed into a round gondola, outfitted with four tons of scientific equipment. For protection, the men wore football helmets borrowed from a local high school.

The trio was already past record heights at 60,000 feet when they heard a fearsome clatter. Wrote Stevens, "We were startled to see a large rip in the balloon's lower surface . . . Through the overhead glass porthole we watched the rent in the fabric gradually

◀ **1934** Just over a year after Major William Kepner (left) kicked Captain Albert W. Stevens free of the plummeting *Explorer I*, Stevens and Captain Orvil Anderson reached the stratosphere and a record altitude of 13.71 miles in *Explorer II* (below) on November 11, 1935. The balloon record held for 21 years.

become larger and larger." Suddenly the bottom of the balloon dropped out, the gondola plunged into free fall, and the men struggled to bail out with their parachutes. Anderson catapulted off into space, but Stevens got stuck halfway through the small hatch of the gondola. Kepner kicked furiously at Stevens's chest to push him out. They were only 300 feet from Earth when they tumbled free and pulled their ripcords. The capsule then crashed into a Nebraska cornfield. Undeterred, Stevens and Anderson lifted off in *Explorer* II only 16 months later and set a balloon altitude record of 72,395 feet that stood for the next 21 years.

Perhaps nothing so exemplified the venture-some spirit of the Geographic as did Luis Marden's quest for the famous ship *Bounty*. Everyone knew that *Bounty* had been sailed by her mutinous crew to Pitcairn Island, a lonely speck in the vast Pacific, and burned and sunk there in 1790. No one,

# WHAT LIES BENEATH

## ARCHAEOLOGY AT NATIONAL GEOGRAPHIC

Lost cities, sunken treasures, ancient mummies: Since the dawn of civilization humans have left fragments of their existence for later generations to uncover and interpret. And while rarely are the finds as exciting as a lost city or a mummy, one quarter of all grants given by the Society's Committee for Research and Exploration support archaeology—the study of past civilizations.

The first archaeological expedition sponsored by the Geographic did cause excitement. In 1913 Hiram Bingham reported in National Geographic the existence of Machu Picchu, an Inca citadel high in the Peruvian Andes. This was followed by the work of Neil Judd, who in the 1920s explored the mysterious Pueblo Bonito, "beautiful village," situated in present-day New Mexico's Chaco Canyon National Monument. And in the forests of Mexico in the 1930s Matthew Stirling found traces of the Olmec, a pre-Columbian civilization whose colossal stone heads, jade necklaces, and mysterious objects are not yet fully understood. Recently Society-supported archaeologists have found royal Moche tombs in Peru, the frozen mummy of the "Inca Ice Maiden," and a staircase covered with hieroglyphs in Honduras. Farther north, in L'Anse aux Meadows, Newfoundland, Helge Ingstad uncovered proof that Norsemen visited the New World five centuries prior to Columbus, while in Virginia, William Kelso excavated the site of James Fort at Jamestown.

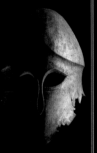

And Egypt, land of the pharaohs, never fails to deliver spectacular treasures. Maynard Owen Williams recorded the breathless opening of Tutankhamun's tomb in 1922. Since then the Society has supported the video camera "excavation" of a pharaonic boat near the Great Pyramid at Giza in the late 1980s and Zahi Hawass as he chronicled his discovery of golden mummies for a TV audience.

These fragments of history are part of our ever expanding human story, one that continues to promise great treasure for those who seek it out. ■

▶ **1957** Fletcher Christian, great-great-grandson of a famous mutineer, negotiates the recovery of the anchor from the *Bounty* at Pitcairn Island.

however, had thought to seek her remains until Luis Marden, on a whim, decided to cross half the globe to find them. Finally arriving at Pitcairn in December 1956, Marden, an early disciple of scuba diving, spent weeks searching fruitlessly in the pounding surf and dangerous currents. Then, in January 1957, near the end of his stay, he spotted an oarlock on the sea bottom, and then a long sandy trench full of what looked like petrified worms—copper sheathing nails marking the former keel of a ship. The wood had long since disappeared, but other bits of hull fittings were nearby. So was the anchor. They were all that remained of Bounty, but they were pieces of a legend.

Marden cabled back to Society headquarters the cryptic message: "Have found the curlew's nest," so that the news services would not scoop the story. In December 1957 "I Found the Bones of the Bounty" was published in National Geographic magazine; it caused an international sensation. Even the motion picture Marden had made was in demand—so much so that it became the first Society film ever broadcast on television.

▲ **1959** A diver recovers a 1,000-year-old Maya jar from a cenote, a natural well in Dzibilchaltún, Mexico, a site excavated by E. Wyllys Andrews of Tulane University.

In 1954 Gilbert H. Grosvenor, the "Geographer to Millions," retired at the age of 78, passing on the editorship to his long-time associate John Oliver La Gorce. Grosvenor had made the Society and its magazine a national institution, but times were changing, and the institution would need to change with them. La Gorce was a caretaker, really, in preparation for the time that Melville Grosvenor "inherited" the office.

The Geographic was not a family-owned business, but neither was it a corporation, and the Board of Trustees was simply acknowledging the talent and leadership of the Grosvenor family. Melville— imbued with grandfather Bell's insatiable curiosity, his father's common touch, and his mother's charm— would be the one who broadened the Society's activities and modernized its magazine in a decade-long expansion.

When Melville became Editor on January 8, 1957, he embraced change

## LUIS MARDEN

O nce described as the epitome of the Geographic man, Luis Marden (1913–2003) was a self-taught scholar, linguist, botanist, navigator, diver, and pilot who pioneered the Society's use of 35-mm color photography. An enthusiastic traveler, Marden roamed most of the world in his more than 40 years as a writer and photographer for the Society.

▲ **1963** Born in a three-week frenzy of activity that produced a guide to Jacqueline Kennedy's refurbished White House (above), the Special Publications division quickly became an important division of the Society. Melville Grosvenor (above, right) presents the finished product on July 4, 1963. One of its editors, Robert L. Breeden, would over the next two decades turn such incipient efforts into an astonishingly successful publishing endeavor that has sold more than 50,000,000 books.

and innovation so that the Society might widen its scope and appeal. Although to some conservative members it verged on sacrilege, in 1959 Melville slapped color pictures on magazine covers that had traditionally been mere tables of contents, framed by a border of oak and laurel leaves. He had an even more ambitious goal: full color in the magazine. When the February 1962 *National Geographic* came off the Society's new state-of-the-art printing presses, there was not a single black-and-white picture in it. The *Geographic* was the first periodical in the U.S. to achieve this technological milestone.

Aware that the Society was regarded as a national institution, Melville emphasized public service as a Society responsibility. First Lady Jacqueline Kennedy was so impressed by a *National Geographic* article on the White House that she persuaded the White House Historical Association to ask the Society to produce an official guidebook to the executive mansion. That request could be accommodated

◀ **1959** Believing photographs on the cover would help identify each issue, Melville Bell Grosvenor broke new ground in September 1959. Irate members complained but soon learned to love the cover photographs.

because the Society had recently launched a new book publishing arm, the Book Service, which complemented the magazine and fed readers' continued hunger for captivating stories and photography.

A soaring new ten-story marble headquarters building, on the corner of 17th and M Streets, was built to hold the growing Society. Explorers Hall, a museum and exhibition space, dominated the ground floor and featured an 11-foot-wide revolving globe. President Lyndon B. Johnson dedicated the new headquarters in 1964, remarking that the "Society had broadened the horizons and narrowed the misunderstandings of many generations."

These were exciting years for the National Geographic Society. Meanwhile, on February 4, 1966, Gilbert Hovey Grosvenor died at the age of 90, never awakening from an afternoon nap. In 1957 he had written about his lifelong labor of love: "But not for youth itself would I trade the treasures stored in my memory: The rich experiences of one who roamed always with a hungry heart, the friendships I have enjoyed with men and women of courage and destiny, and, above all, the immeasurable satisfaction of seeing the National Geographic Society and its magazine surpass my every dream." ∎

# DID YOU WATCH
## THE GEOGRAPHIC
# LAST NIGHT?

*"Challenge and inspiration are the greatest treasures from the sea. We are just beginning to learn her science, art, and philosophy and how to live in her embrace."*

**JACQUES COUSTEAU**

◄ **1960s** A filmmaker treads gingerly along a glacial deposit to shoot footage for one of the Society's first Television Specials, *Alaska!*, which aired on CBS in 1967. National Geographic Television Specials heralded the dawn of a new era for the Society. By the end of the 1960s the Specials had become highly anticipated events.

1964 With one touch of nature, Jane Goodall and newborn Flint made the whole world kin.

In 1963 the National Geographic Society reached the top of the world. On May 22 Barry Bishop of the magazine staff planted the Society's flag on the summit of Mount Everest. Bishop was a member of the first American team—and one of the first groups to summit the world's tall-est mountain. His feat crowned the Society's 75th anniversary. For three-quarters of a century the Geographic had grown ever larger until its membership now topped three million. As its staff prepared to move into the new marble head-quarters building, the Society released its first world atlas, long dreamed of and seven years in the actual making. Melville Grosvenor deemed it the Society's

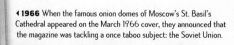

◄ **1966** When the famous onion domes of Moscow's St. Basil's Cathedral appeared on the March 1966 cover, they announced that the magazine was tackling a once taboo subject: the Soviet Union.

"largest, handsomest and most ambitious contribution to Geographic knowledge." Never in history had so many opportunities beckoned. President Kennedy had promised to explore the stars and tap the ocean depths. Science and exploration were expanding at a rapid pace—and the National Geographic Society looked for new ways to bring the world to its readers. Photographic and printing innovations allowed *National Geographic* to explode with color. Whatever the subject—the Italian Riviera, New Guinea tribesmen, hummingbirds, or sleek jet aircraft—it was presented in dynamic new layouts. Vivid illustrations splashed across the cover. Melville Grosvenor tripled the photographic budget and hired a bright new staff of photographers and writers with fresh ideas.

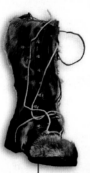

▲ **1963** Leather-and-fur boots worn by Barry Bishop for the 1963 ascent of Mount Everest

Nor was that all. The Society's lecture program, featuring narrated films, had long been a popular Washington institution. But Grosvenor saw in the advent of color television the perfect platform for carrying such films to the nation at large. On September 10, 1965, the Society aired its first Television Special. *Americans on Everest* made an astonishing impact, receiving the highest ratings of any documentary broadcast to that time. Soon four Specials a year were not only elevating the standards of the format but they also were regularly attracting large audiences. By 1968, when *Amazon* aired, it drew 35 million viewers, more viewers than any other show on television in a two-week period.

▲ **1959** Densely packed color and dynamic layouts on almost every page showcased the power of color photography in the 1950s and '60s.

The Geographic's heroes of old had been intrepid explorers and frostbitten gentlemen framed in the magazine's oak and

▲ **1959** Jacques Cousteau received 37 grants from the Society. A staff artist commemorated one of his visits with the caricature at right, drawn in the Society's official guest book.

▲ **1962** *Men, Ships, and the Sea,* by Alan Villiers, chronicled the history of sail.

laurel. But such Television Specials as *Miss Goodall and the Wild Chimpanzees, Dr. Leakey and the Dawn of Man,* and *The World of Jacques Cousteau* brought new heroes, emerging from specialized fields of science, into every living room.

Few captured the popular imagination as did Frenchman Jacques Cousteau. Charismatic and visionary, Cousteau had co-developed the Aqua-Lung, the first true underwater breathing device, which opened up a whole new realm for exploration. But he was little known outside France until the Geographic in 1952 began sponsoring his projects. Working from his famous research vessel, *Calypso,* Cousteau then pioneered new underwater filming techniques with strobe inventor Harold Edgerton.

He developed a rudderless diving saucer that could maneuver with thruster nozzles like an underwater airplane. He built a series of undersea dwellings named Conshelf, proving that humans could live and work for long periods beneath the waves. Over the years he took readers with him through a dozen popular articles in National Geographic And the success of the Society's 1966 Television Special eventually led Cousteau to develop his own long-running television series.

The Aqua-Lung had permitted archaeologist George Bass of the University of Pennsylvania to systematically excavate—on the seabed—both Bronze Age and Byzantine-era shipwrecks, lying deep off the coast of southern Turkey. Supported by the Society, Bass pioneered the science of underwater archaeology and would eventually contribute a half dozen accounts of his work to National Geographic.

**1960s** Using the grid techniques of classical archaeology, George Bass almost single-handedly pioneered the science of underwater archaeology.

**1960s** A longtime Society grantee, Bass reported on his Byzantine-era shipwreck excavation that yielded this earthenware plate and cup for the July 1963 *Geographic*.

In 1959 the Society began sponsoring the work of Louis and Mary Leakey, who had long been probing Tanzania's Olduvai Gorge for traces of human origins. Their discovery of the fossil remains of a 1.8-million-year-old hominid had opened up tremendous new vistas in paleoanthropology. Digging in the exposed cliffs of the eroded gorge the couple collected bone fragments, stone tools, and bits of extinct animals pointing to Africa as the likely cradle of humankind. Louis Leakey, with his tousled white hair and mischievous grin, was made familiar to millions through National Geographic articles and the Society's 1966 Television Special.

Louis Leakey believed he could gain insight into early man by studying the great apes. He

▲ **1961** Louis and Mary Leakey and son Philip examine a 1.7-million-year-old campsite in Tanzania's Olduvai Gorge. The "First Family of Paleoanthropology," the Leakeys—three generations of them—have also excavated fossils from Kenya's Lake Turkana region. Their work was pivotal in proving Africa to be the cradle of humanity.

▶ **1968** Flo, matriarch of one of Gombe's chimpanzee clans, cradles daughter Flame while son Flint exhibits a recognizably human jealousy.

encouraged a trio of fascinating and courageous women to dedicate their careers to primates. Jane Goodall, a soft-spoken young Englishwoman, virtually lived with the chimpanzees frequenting Tanzania's Gombe National Game Reserve. There she made the startling discovery that chimps often fashioned simple tools. Goodall's long relationship with the Society led to numerous articles and television Specials. The classic photograph of a chimp reaching out to touch Goodall's hand with his extended forefinger has become a symbol of our deep kinship with the natural world.

The second researcher, Dian Fossey, left the U.S. in 1967 with a grant from the Society to study mountain gorillas. In the remote Rwandan forests

she soon made observations revealing that gorillas were not ferocious apes but rather shy and gentle creatures. Her own reputation for ferocity, however—she practically waged a one-woman war against poachers—led to her being murdered in 1985. Meanwhile, in the rain forests of Borneo, Biruté Galdikas had in 1971 embarked on a study of orangutans, which the Society supported for many years.

Closer to home, twin brothers Frank and John Craighead advanced wildlife biology by developing radio-tracking devices for large animals. In the August 1960 National Geographic they described their efforts, undertaken with Society support, to immobilize Yellowstone grizzly bears with anesthetic darts to safely measure, weigh, and study the powerful animals. Soon they began fitting them with radio-transmitting collars and tracked the bears' wanderings and monitored their physiology not only via handheld receivers but also eventually by satellite, gaining a better understanding of grizzly habits and behavior. The exciting moments in this work were vividly captured in a 1967 Television Special. These techniques have since become important tools in wildlife studies, used around the globe to study animals from elephants to whales to bats.

The Society had never failed to endorse the preservation of wilderness and natural beauty. The July 1966 National Geographic commemorated the 50th anniversary of the National Park Service by showcasing the existing 32 parks. It also urged the creation of a new one. California's magnificent coast redwood groves were threatened with logging. A Society grant had enabled the Park Service to determine

## ALL IN THE FAMILY

Under the blazing African sun, three generations of Leakeys have studied the fossils of early man. Louis S. B. Leakey, a maverick thinker, encountered scorn from mainstream paleoanthropologists in the 1950s when he first insisted that Africa, not Asia, was the cradle of mankind. But at Olduvai Gorge in 1959, Louis's wife, Mary, discovered a 1.8-million-year-old skull that was the oldest hominid fossil then found. More discoveries soon followed, including 3.6-million-year-old hominid footprints left in hardened lava at nearby Laetoli. Continuing the family business, their son Richard led numerous fossil-finding expeditions around Kenya's Lake Turkana, where the camp at Koobi Fora is now directed by his wife, Meave, and daughter Louise, currently National Geographic explorers-in-residence.

# NATIONAL PARKS

## A TRADITION OF CONSERVATION

▸ **1925** A fantastic vista of stalagmites dominates the bizarre underworld of New Mexico's Carlsbad Caverns in this 1920s-era photograph.

▾ **1915** Joined in a protective circle, a 1915 party rings a California giant sequoia. National Geographic has long worked to protect natural treasures.

L egend has it that a visiting Englishman once described the national parks as "the best idea America ever had." The National Geographic Society has certainly thought it a good enough idea that for most of its history it has been showcasing the parks through words and pictures, books, magazine articles, maps, and films. Society leaders helped organize the National Park Service, and Society efforts have saved endangered tracts of Sequoia National Park and helped establish Redwood and Shenandoah National Parks.

National Geographic Society field expeditions have explored, mapped, and photographed many areas of sublime scenery that, brought to the world's attention through the magazine, were also considered worthy of incorporation into the park system. That's how the spectacular Valley of Ten Thousand Smokes in Alaska became part of Katmai National Monument, and how an extraordinary cave system in New Mexico was designated Carlsbad Caverns National Park. In the 1950s Society-supported archaeologists excavated 1,500-year-old Native American artifacts from a cave in Alabama. It duly became Russell Cave National Monument. And elsewhere in the world, Gombe National Park in Tanzania and Gabon's national park system owe much to Society-supported research projects. ∎

an area that should be safeguarded. A Society team then found in that area the world's tallest tree, scraping the sky at over 367 feet. And the July 1966 issue exhorted members to lobby Congress to preserve the forests. "Today . . . redwoods make a last stand against the inroads of man," wrote Melville Bell Grosvenor. Such efforts proved fruitful: In 1968 Redwood National Park was officially established.

A startled nation awoke to the space age when the Soviet Union launched the Sputnik satellite in 1957. Even before President Kennedy vowed to put an astronaut on the moon by the end of the decade, National Geographic had loaned staff photographer Dean Conger to NASA to make a permanent color record of the manned space program. Conger's pictures of astronaut Alan Shepard, the first American in space, being plucked from the ocean, appeared in newspapers around the world. When in 1962 John Glenn became

▲ **1960** Brothers Frank and John Craighead employed innovative techniques in radio-tracking wildlife, particularly grizzly bears. Passionate defenders of wildlife, they wrote, "Restoring and maintaining a healthy world ecology depends on man's ability to understand and to respect nature in all her diversity . . . Our future lies in the heart and mind of man."

▸ **1966** Celebrating the 50th anniversary of the National Park Service, in July 1966 National Geographic made a pointed call for the establishment of California's Redwood National Park.

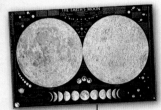

▲ **1969** In one of its most challenging cartographic accomplishments, the Society's "Map of the Moon," published in the February 1969 *National Geographic*, was the first popular map to show the entire lunar surface, including its mysterious far side, on a single sheet.

▶ **1961** Having just completed the first spaceflight made by an American, astronaut Alan Shepard is pulled from the Atlantic into a Navy helicopter. Photographer Dean Conger mounted a camera above the helicopter door that, firing repeatedly, happened to make this stunning shot. Striving to document this most enthralling of adventures, Society photographers like Conger, Luis Marden, and Otis Imboden shared their unrivaled expertise in color photography with both astronauts and NASA technicians.

the first American to orbit the Earth, he carried a tiny Geographic flag, and National Geographic photographers made historic photos of the launch and recovery.

Neil Armstrong also carried a small National Geographic flag when in July 1969 he became the first person to step on the surface of the moon. In December of that year, the magazine published a five-part package on the feat, not only printing the historic words and photographs of the mission but also including a small phonographic record, *Sounds of the Space Age*. Ken Weaver, science editor at the time,

wrote, "No one who sat that July night welded to his TV screen will ever forget the sight of that ghostly foot groping slowly past the ladder to Eagle's footpad, and then stepping tentatively onto the virgin soil."

Beyond the moon the planets beckoned, and beyond the planets, the Milky Way galaxy. Into those great unexplored regions NASA hurled its unmanned, instrument-laden probes. Soon the faces of Mercury, Venus, and Mars—once known only as stars in the sky—were seen up close in the pages of National Geographic. The Society, using data relayed from the probes, produced a map of Mars in 1973, and published historic photos of the Martian surface made by the Viking spacecraft in 1976.

NASA launched two Voyager spacecraft in 1977 that transmitted millions of images of Jupiter, Saturn, and Uranus. Aboard each vessel was a gold-plated record containing sounds and scenes of Earth, encoded as digital pulses. Intermingled with strains of Bach, Mozart, and Louis Armstrong, with the cry of a chimpanzee and the song of a humpback whale, were 16 images provided by the National Geographic Society—including snowflakes, a Balinese dancer, cresting dolphins, the Great Wall of China—images diffusing geographic knowledge to the cosmos.

Science holds a particular fascination for readers, and National Geographic earned a reputation for clear presentation of complex topics and difficult

▲ **1949** Astronomer Edwin Hubble at Mount Palomar Observatory in California. Hubble championed what became the National Geographic–Mount Palomar Sky Survey (1949–1956), a colossal photomapping of the night sky from the Northern Hemisphere, which made an enormous contribution to 20th-century astronomy.

◀ **1961** Astronaut Alan Shepard and photographer Dean Conger share a friendly chat.

subjects in an easily accessible manner, fully illustrated with diagrams and maps. "You and the Obedient Atom" a 1958 article, demonstrated that the atomic age need not be associated only with mushroom clouds but might also bring immense benefits to everyday life. "The Laser's Bright Magic," a 1966 story, graphically depicted the nature and potential of that "sword of light." Readers quickly came to rely on the Geographic's science coverage for information about the latest technologies.

In 1957 the International Geophysical Year (IGY) began, a program of worldwide studies embracing land, sea, and sky in an effort to learn more about Earth as a single functioning system. Many countries were involved, and Lyman J. Briggs, chairman of the Society's Research Committee, was a key member of the U.S. organizing committee. Nearly a dozen articles in National Geographic profiled various aspects of the program. A number of Society-funded research projects had specific IGY applications, especially the cosmic ray investigations conducted by Martin Pomerantz.

Back on Earth, National Geographic did not shrink from

▲ **1979** Voyager 1 approaching Jupiter

▶ **1953** Explaining the glories of the uranium atom to students

▼ **1930s–1960s** 35-mm rangefinder cameras like this Leica were favorites with photographers between the late 1930s and early 1960s.

covering the war in Vietnam. Wilbur E. (Bill) Garrett, a dynamic picture editor from Missouri, shot gritty photographs of that conflict, which continued pushing a harder-hitting photojournalism into the magazine's once staid pages. Staff writer Peter White's reports ranged from Saigon to the Mekong Delta to villages and rice paddies. Staff photographer Emory Kristof caught a mortar fragment in his eye while covering a Thanksgiving Day patrol. And freelance photographer Dickey Chappelle contributed pictures and stories before becoming the first American female correspondent killed in action.

Science and photojournalism notwithstanding, National Geographic always reserved room for starry-eyed adventurers. Among them was Melville Bell Grosvenor himself, who above all else loved to rove the sea. Under his touch, the magazine thrummed to the billow and snap of sail. His own articles describing voyages in his yacht, White Mist, were enormously popular. So were those of the great sailor Alan Villiers, whose

# BECAUSE IT IS THERE

MOUNTAINEERING AT THE GEOGRAPHIC

▲ **1966** Nicholas
Clinch battles his
way to the summit
of Vinson Massif,
Antarctica's high-
est peak, in 1966.
Clinch led National
Geographic's
American Antarctic
Expedition, which
became the first to
climb Antarctica's
highest peaks,
located in the
Sentinel Range
of the Ellsworth
Mountains.

"Because it is there." The answer to the question—
"why?"—asked of George Mallory when he sought to
become the first person to climb Mount Everest is a
poignant expression of the irresistible lure of mountains,
which has played a major role in the Society's history.

Though Israel Russell did not reach the summit of
Mount St. Elias on the Society's first expedition in 1890, his
thrilling account of the attempt filled the May 1891 issue of
the magazine. Mountaineering, essential to determining the
geography of many unknown places, was an important component of subsequent expeditions, including Robert Griggs's
expedition to Alaska's Valley of Ten Thousand Smokes,
where he achieved the first summit of Mount Katmai.

Mountaineering legend Bradford Washburn led a 1935 Society expedition to the Yukon in which he mapped more than 5,000 square miles of territory previously marked "unknown" on the map. Washburn and his wife, Barbara, circled the globe, completing the most detailed maps of the Grand Canyon and Mount Everest ever created. In 1998, at age 88, Washburn directed the efforts of a team that used GPS to calculate the precise height of Everest, adding seven feet to the world's tallest mountain.

▲ 1941 Barbara and Brad Washburn stand atop Alaska's Mount Hayes.

The Society awarded Edmund Hillary and Tenzing Norgay the Hubbard Medal for making the first ascent of Everest in 1953. Ten years later the Society helped sponsor the first American expedition to the summit. In 1978 the *Geographic* published Reinhold Messner's account of the first ascent of Everest without oxygen. Messner went on to climb all 14 of the world's 8,000-meter peaks without oxygen. Society grantee Ed Viesturs, the first American to match Messner's feat, aided in the rescue effort for 11 climbers lost on Everest in 1996, a tragedy documented in the book *Into Thin Air.*

▼ 1963 A pair of protective goggles and an ice pick, important tools of the mountaineer's trade

In 2002 the Society sponsored a different kind of mountain expedition. Conrad Anker, Rick Ridgeway, Galen Rowell, and Jimmy Chin traveled to Tibet's remote Chang Tang region to confirm the birthing grounds of the endangered chiru, an antelope prized for its wool. They alerted officials to the threats faced by these delicate creatures and the rugged landscape they call home. ∎

**1966** "Like a vision from the heroic days of sail, she rose up from the dark-blue shield of the Pacific . . ." The brigantine *Yankee*, described by Luis Marden, made globe-girdling voyages with crews of teenagers.

pen oozed brine. He capped off his Geographic contributions with the best-selling book *Men, Ships, and the Sea*, filled with tales of Magellan, Drake, and other great seafarers. Year in and year out, Irving Johnson sailed his storied *Yankee* all over the globe, and readers of the magazine followed his adventures. If they also watched the 1966 Television Special *Voyage of the Brigantine Yankee*, they heard for the first time the trumpet fanfare that would become the Geographic's television signature.

**1969** Marking the apogee of human exploration, the December 1969 *National Geographic* featured five different articles about the historic moon landing as well as a record, *Sounds of the Space Age*.

But no one seemed to captivate readers as did an adventurous schoolboy, Robin Lee Graham, who sailed alone out of Los Angeles one July day in 1965 in a 24-foot fiberglass sloop named Dove. When he returned, 1,739 days and 30,000 nautical miles later, he had a new wife, a new sloop, and legions of admiring fans enthralled by his three National Geographic articles. "Why did I choose to sail around the world?" Graham wrote. "I want to see the world, and not on a tourist's itinerary with a passport stamped full of one-day visas. No, my passport must be imprinted with memories of landfalls where foreigners seldom set foot."

▼ **1968** Robin Lee Graham charts his solo course around the world.

As its skipper for ten years, Melville Bell Grosvenor had steered the National Geographic Society in many new directions. Its magazines, books, and television programs were reaching out in new ways to new audiences while retaining that glorious photography and distinctive style of storytelling. Yet it was all perhaps too splendid. "The world of National Geographic is usually a sunlit Kodachrome world of altruistic human achievement in settings of natural beauty," carped one Newsweek reporter. Its "traditional tone of gentlemanly detachment from the ugliness, misery, and strife of the world" was belittled by the New York Times. In the coming years the Society would have to confront such criticisms and see the world with a more appraising eye. New landfalls still lay ahead. ∎

▼ **1959** Melville Bell Grosvenor, President and Editor of the National Geographic Society between 1957 and 1967, at Angkor Wat.

# LIVING WITH THE PLANET

*"When you realize the value
of all life, you dwell less
on what is past and
concentrate more on the
preservation of the future."*

**DIAN FOSSEY**

◀ **1977** Digit, a Rwandan mountain gorilla studied by Dian Fossey, a National Geographic Society grantee and protégé of Louis Leakey. Fossey, whose work in the 1970s and '80s did much to dispel myths about the ferocious nature of these creatures, was murdered at her research camp in 1985.

**1981** The stump of Mount St. Helens still smolders nearly a year after its May 18, 1980, eruption. The January 1981 *National Geographic* article on the cataclysm became one of the most popular stories in the magazine's history.

▲ **1977** Sunlight filters through a fragile Eden of ancient trees in California's Redwood National Park. Some of the trees are more than 400 years old and stand taller than the Statue of Liberty.

◀ **1970** Environmental issues took center stage in the December issue of *National Geographic*, which featured extended coverage of "Our Ecological Crisis."

By the early 1970s National Geographic appeared to be the same dynamic, multifaceted place it had always been. An ever widening circle of writers, photographers, scientists, and explorers still set out into the field, returning months later with new discoveries, striking photographs, and exciting stories. National Geographic magazine, maps, books, lectures, and television programs were reaching an audience of millions.

Nevertheless, there was a new look to the magazine's pages. Staff photographers still won international acclaim for their work, but alongside their pictures of lush landscapes and colorful costumes were depictions of squalor, strife, misery, and pollution. "It was a different

game for us," *Geographic* photographer James Blair remarked, "to not look for something beautiful, but for something awful."

Blair's memorable picture of the dank water and rusted mills of Cleveland's Cuyahoga River, so befouled by oil and debris that it actually caught fire in 1969, appeared in the December 1970 issue. The article "Pollution, Threat to Man's Only Home" marked a turning point at the magazine. The *Geographic* had always addressed natural history subjects. Birds had long been a popular staple, as were articles by Paul Zahl, staff naturalist, who took his family with him in a succession of wood-paneled station wagons in quest of natural curiosities. But by the late 1960s a powerful new force had swept across the nation: the environmental movement.

Slowly, then rapidly, the *Geographic* embraced the new perspective. For the next two decades the magazine that once pictured hunting trips and specimen collecting in Africa and Asia instead drew attention to the plight of elephants, pandas, rhinoceroses, and whales. It documented the ravages of pollution and summarized the challenges of pesticides, nuclear power, and acid rain. Remaining strictly impartial, it presented all sides of complex technological and ecological issues. National Geographic was presenting readers the same beautiful world, but seen in another light.

It was a different game, after all, one fit for a new generation rising at the Society. In 1970 another member of its leading family

▲ **1970** A three-page foldout of Ohio's devastated Cuyahoga River in the December issue epitomizes the magazine's new direction. In 1969 the river had become so polluted with oil that it actually caught fire, destroying two railroad bridges.

▲ **1970s** The Nikon 35-mm single-lens reflex was the camera of choice by the 1970s. Digital SLRs are photojournalists' preferred tools today.

▲ **1970s** Photographers began documenting an imperfect world in the 1970s, shooting this scene of violence in a Palestinian market (above) and apartheid in South Africa (right). Increased coverage of controversial subjects was thought risky by some, but Editor Gilbert M. Grosvenor was vindicated when Society membership grew at a faster rate than ever before. By 1980, the Society had more than ten million members.

stepped to the fore when Gilbert M. Grosvenor, Melville's son, became the Editor of National Geographic. Stung by criticisms that the magazine presented too rosy a view of the world, Gil Grosvenor weighed his grandfather's rules specifying that only things of "a kindly nature" and "nothing partisan or controversial" should appear in its pages. He determined to be fair but unflinching, promising that the Geographic would be not only a mirror to the world but also "a mirror of its times, reflecting the changes through which we pass."

Thus turmoil in Africa, the Middle East, and Central America was soon reflected in the magazine. As Cold War tensions started to lessen, Geographic writers and photographers explored

China, North Korea, Cuba, and the Soviet Union—communist strongholds often shunned by earlier editors. Articles depicting poverty in Harlem and apartheid in South Africa raised eyebrows. Some thought such controversial stories and the new environmental emphasis smacked of advocacy journalism. But Grosvenor answered skeptics by insisting that "the magazine is not changing, the world is changing."

Meanwhile, other Society branches also budded in new directions. Educational and book publishing flourished. Maps broadened their scope to include relevant cultural and historical information. And in 1975, the Society launched World magazine for 8- to 14-year-olds, which soon was reaching 1.3 million youngsters.

In the field Society-supported scientists were also seeking to understand this changing world. Biologists studied not only animals but their rapidly disappearing habitats as well. Dr. George Schaller trekked into the high mountains of South Asia to examine populations of wild sheep, goats, and the rare snow leopard. Eugenie Clark, the "Shark Lady," was transforming our

▲ **1975** With its debut, World magazine brought the stories and images of National Geographic to a younger audience. The magazine continues today as National Geographic Kids.

▼ **1977** Written and photographed by black freelancers, the article "To Live in Harlem" was a milestone: the magazine's first coverage of black Americans.

▲ **1985** Eugenie Clark struggles to untangle two six-gilled sharks and a gummy shark caught on the same fishing longline.

▼ **1979** *Songs of the Humpback Whale* was inserted into the January *Geographic*.

▶ **1971** Trekking miles through remote Asia, biologist George Schaller shot the first images of the elusive snow leopard in the wild.

understanding of sharks. Often disdaining steel "shark cages," she swam freely among these mysterious, fascinating creatures. At the same time, Roger Payne was studying the humpback whale. A record of their haunting "songs" was bound into each copy of the January 1979 issue of National Geographic.

In Mexico's Sierra Madre naturalist Fred Urquhart solved a long-standing mystery when his team discovered the previously unknown wintering grounds of the eastern North American butterfly. Katherine Payne, working in Kenya in the late 1980s, revealed that elephants, endangered by heavy poaching, communicate through infrasonic sounds, low-pitched rumblings carrying for miles across the landscape. Meanwhile,

as Jane Goodall, Dian Fossey, and Biruté Galdikas continued demonstrating the close kinship between apes and humans, Francine (Penny) Patterson showed that an endangered lowland gorilla named Koko possessed marked linguistic skills. Geographic articles, books, and a Television Special, *Search for the Great Apes*, brought the stories of these important projects to the world.

These explorers had all been championed by Melvin M. Payne, Society President between 1967 and 1976, whose sharp eye for promising scientists matched his firm grip on business affairs. A strong proponent of field research, Payne himself spent many months "under canvas" and was awarded the Conservation Service Medal, the Interior Department's highest honor, for his "leadership in exploration, research, and education."

In 1980, Gil Grosvenor gave up the editorship to become the Society's President. The creative and energetic Bill Garrett then became Editor of National Geographic. A magazine that had already grown to include subjects as disparate as rats and the Shroud of Turin now broadened even further. Articles ranged from the archaeology of garbage to the mystery of sleep to the sense of smell, complete with a scratch-and-sniff card to test readers' responses to key odors. Staff photographer James Stanfield negotiated the mazes of the Vatican and emerged with exclusive coverage. Garrett also published a series of three-dimensional holographic covers, the first to appear on a mass-circulation magazine.

Above all, photojournalism flourished. Steve McCurry, a gutsy freelance photographer, brought back pictures of

▲ **1975** A mystery solved: Biologist Fred Urquhart discovered the wintering grounds of the eastern population of monarch butterflies.

▼ **1971** Named in honor of its discoverer, this rare orchid was found in Brazil by staff member Luis Marden.

# PAGE BY PAGE

## MAKING THE MAGAZINE

▸ **1998** Sporting 3-D glasses, editorial staff attend a "wall walk," examining 3-D photographs of Mars that were subsequently published in August 1998.

▾ **1980s** Checked and rechecked and checked still again, a marked-up text proof vividly demonstrates the Research Division's scrupulous regard for accuracy.

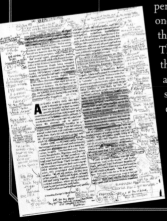

It starts as an idea, a story proposal on, let's pretend, Shangri-La, approved by the magazine's planning council. A writer and a photographer are then assigned and dispatched to this mythical land. Many weeks later, after fieldwork is done, illustrations editors comb through the resulting photographs, perhaps as many as 20,000, to find just the right ones, at most only several dozen, that best illustrate the story. Layout proceeds and text is polished. The article is rigorously checked for accuracy by the Research Division. The Editor always personally picks the cover picture. The finest paper and state-of-the-art presses then ensure the highest quality printing. Finally, anywhere from several months to several years after it first began as an idea, members find in their mailboxes the *Geographic*'s latest on that place that is no-place, Shangri-La. ∎

▲ **1985** Gaining unprecedented access to the Vatican in 1985, photographer Jim Stanfield gave readers a rare glimpse of the pope alone in his garden, away from the crowds that followed his every movement.

war-torn Afghanistan and the drought-stricken Sahel of Africa. Prizewinning writer Mike Edwards and photographer Steve Raymer covered the tragedy of the Chernobyl nuclear accident in 1987. And in what would become the most popular article in *National Geographic* history, Rowe Findley related the gripping story of Mount St. Helens's eruption in 1981. "The shining Sunday morning turns forebodingly gray and to a blackness in which a hand cannot be seen in front of an eye. In the eerie gray and black, relieved only by jabs of lightning, filled with thunder and abrading winds, a thousand desperate acts of search and salvation are underway."

Meanwhile, explorers and adventurers pressed on in the old-fashioned way, one foot after another. In

▶ **1985** The iconic face of a war-torn Afghan refugee first appeared on the cover of the May 1985 issue. Her identity remained a mystery until 2002, when her name was discovered to be Sharbat Gula.

▲ **1988** Staff photographer Bruce Dale spent weeks exploding the globe on the holographic cover for the December 1988 cover.

▸ **1979** Hurricane David blasts Miami Beach.

▾ **1981** Coverage of the cataclysmic eruption of Mount St. Helens in 1981 captured readers' attention like no other story in the magazine's history.

ST. HELENS
## MOUNTAIN WITH A DEATH WISH

A gleaming white peak in the Cascades blasts away the top 1,300 feet of its crest in a massive eruption that takes dozens of lives, perils 200 square miles, triggers floods and mudflows, and sends ash clouds rolling across the Northeast. Twenty-two photographers capture the cataclysm in broad scope and stunning detail, and Assistant Editor Rowe Findley writes an intensely personal, three-part account of this first volcanic event in the contiguous 48 states in 63 years.

1977 Peter and Barbara Jenkins completed a walk across America. That same year, Robyn Davidson and four camels crossed 1,700 miles of Australian outback. In 1986 polar explorer Will Steger completed the first successful unresupplied dogsled expedition to the North Pole since Peary's 1909 trip. And in 1980, armed with little more than ski poles and an ice ax, Reinhold Messner became the first person to summit Everest without

bottled oxygen. Messner wrote in the October 1981 National Geographic, "I want to experience the mountain as it really is … By using an artificial oxygen supply, I feel I would no longer be climbing the mountain towering above me. I would simply be bringing its summit down to me."

Pluck and daring and originality of mind led legendary adventurer Thor Heyerdahl, author of Kon-Tiki, to risk ocean voyages in boats made solely of papyrus reeds. Those same qualities plus a love of story compelled Tim Severin to sail a leather boat from Ireland to Newfoundland, imitating sixth-century Irish monk St. Brendan, and to follow in the imaginary wakes of Ulysses, Jason, and Sinbad. Readers of the magazine learned how such voyages proved the capabilities of ancient mariners. National Geographic

▲ **1977** Covering communism, photographer Dean Conger captured this parade through Leningrad's Palace Square in celebration of the October 1917 revolution.

▼ **1977** Tom Canby and Jim Stanfield sampled a fried version of their subject for a 1977 story about the adaptable, resilient, and sometimes repulsive rat.

▲ **1985** Stopped for eternity, a pocket watch recovered shortly after *Titanic* sank records the moment of tragedy.

▶ **1991** Illuminated by the Russian *Mir 1* submersible, the bow of the R.M.S. *Titanic* looms out of the deep.

▶ **1988** From a secret chamber in the tomb of a Moche lord, perhaps the finest example of pre-Columbian jewelry ever found emerged in 1988. The figurine at the center of this gold and turquoise ear ornament wears a headdress and an owls' head necklace and has a war club. A skeleton found nearby wore similar attire.

Associate Editor Joseph Judge and the remarkable Luis Marden retraced the path of Christopher Columbus across the Atlantic, conjecturing that tiny Samana Cay in the Bahamas, and not the nearby island of San Salvador, the generally accepted site, was the great explorer's first landfall in the New World.

Exciting discoveries continued to be made. Marine geologist Robert Ballard explored the utter darkness of the deep sea in the Woods Hole Oceanographic Institution's submersible *Alvin*. In 1977, with National Geographic photographic assistance, he found off the Galápagos Islands hydrothermal vents—hot-water springs—in the seafloor. Clustered around the vents were giant clams and tube worms—the first life ever discovered dependent on the Earth's fiery core for energy and not ultimately on the sun.

In 1985 Ballard made another amazing discovery.

"I cannot believe my eyes," he wrote in the December 1985 National Geographic. "From the abyss two and a half miles beneath the sea the bow of a great vessel emerges in ghostly detail." It was the remains of Titanic, the most exciting shipwreck discovery of the time. Around the world, Bob Ballard became a household name.

Society-supported expeditions in East Africa continued to unearth tantalizing traces of our oldest ancestors. Richard Leakey discovered in Kenya a nearly complete skeleton of Homo erectus, our most immediate progenitor. Donald Johanson excavated in Ethiopia a treasure trove of Australopithecus afarensis fossils, perhaps three million years old, representing what may be one of the earliest branches on the human evolutionary tree. And Mary Leakey found fossilized hominid footprints in ancient Tanzanian volcanic ash that she dated at 3.6 million years old—evidence that human ancestors walked on two legs eons earlier than once thought.

While National Geographic published arresting photographs of the recently exhumed dead at Herculaneum, destroyed by the volcano Mount Vesuvius in A.D. 79, other archaeologists studied Aphrodisias, a Greco-Roman city in Turkey. Grantee Christopher Donnan discovered untouched royal Inca tombs in Peru, and Norman Hammond found Maya ones in Belize. One site, Hammond told readers, had all the makings of a childhood fantasy. "An ancient city lost under the green canopy

▼ **1985** Entombed by the eruption that buried Pompeii in A.D. 79, this Roman woman's skeleton was discovered at nearby Herculaneum and featured on the cover of National Geographic in July 1985. Among the woman's treasures were two golden rings, a pair of pierced earrings, and the solid-gold snake-headed bracelets above.

# Under the Sea

## EXPLORING THE OCEAN REALM

▲ **1989** In the shadow of Japan's Mount Fuji the robot SeaROVER dips beneath the surface of Suruga Bay, which plunges to 8,000 meters. Photographers David Doubilet and Emory Kristof and marine biologist Eugenie Clark studied Suruga in 1989, recording the largest creature ever seen in the deep sea: a 23-foot sleeper shark.

he best way to observe fish is to become a fish," said underwater pioneer Jacques Cousteau. Before Cousteau, large portions of Earth's vast oceans were largely unknown. National Geographic has devoted many grants and thousands of pages to attempts to develop the technologies that allow us to become more like fish and learn about the sea.

In 1960, shortly after Cousteau's accounts of underwater exploration with scuba equipment began appearing in the magazine, U.S. Navy Lt. Don Walsh and Jacques Piccard descended seven and a half miles in the bathyscaphe *Trieste* to the deepest spot in the ocean—the Mariana Trench. No one returned for 52 years. But in March 2012, with National Geographic support, filmmaker James Cameron made the first solo dive to that same dark region.

The decades in between have seen great advances in oceanography. In addition to Cousteau the Society supported Edwin Link, who led a series of experiments to test man's ability to live and work in the deep ocean.

The topography of the ocean floor remained virtually unknown until Bruce Heezen and Marie Tharp completed a map of the ocean floor in the 1960s. The map revealed ridges and contours as rugged as any landscape on Earth. Even though it was mapped, much remained to be discovered. The Society participated in the deep-ocean experiments of Project FAMOUS, which made the first manned descents to the Mid-Atlantic Ridge. A young oceanographer named Robert Ballard took part in this expedition and went on to lead another in 1977 to the Galápagos Rift where he discovered the first forms of life based not on photosynthesis but on chemosynthesis. Convinced that remotely operated vehicles could use sonar to view larger portions of the ocean floor, Ballard began developing the technologies that would lead to the discovery of Titanic in 1985. Since then he has gone on to find numerous wrecks and traces of an ancient, cataclysmic flood in the Black Sea.

As quickly as they are being explored, the world's oceans are also being destroyed. Noted marine biologists and explorers-in-residence Sylvia Earle and Enric Sala have been persuading governments to preserve some of the world's remaining pristine coral reefs. The fight to protect our ocean realm continues. ■

# Oases of Life in the Cold Abyss

By JOHN B. CORLISS, Ph.D.
and ROBERT D. BALLARD, Ph.D.

▲ **1979** Robert Ballard's discovery of life at deep-sea vents was announced in the January 1979 *Geographic.*

◀ **1960s** The globe shows the topography of the ocean floor.

▼ **1979** Sylvia Earle descended to a record depth of 1,250 feet in this special "Jim" suit.

▲ **1984** Thousands of letters from Society members over the years inquired about travel to the destinations featured in *National Geographic* magazine. *National Geographic Traveler* launched in 1984. Within a year, subscriptions topped one million.

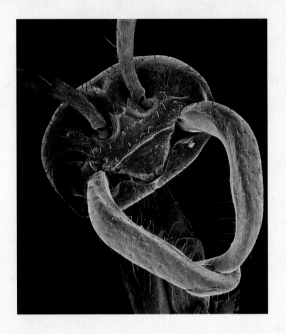

▸ **1974** This army ant is magnified 40 times its actual size under a scanning electron microscope.

▾ **1984** Art with a purpose: The beautiful diagrams and cutaways below visually explain the complicated structure of a strand of DNA.

of a remote jungle. Vines and roots snaking over temples and pyramids. And beneath it all, an undiscovered tomb containing the art of a vanished civilization and the skeletal remains of a long-dead nobleman."

New technologies—remote sensing, lasers, computer graphics, x-rays, and CT scans—allowed the Geographic to picture the world in new ways. One television documentary,

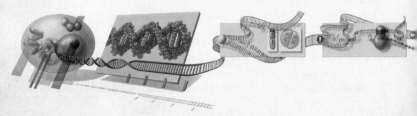

◀ **1970** A National Geographic film crew gets up close and personal for a Special about Ethiopia's crocodiles.

The Invisible World, even showed an image, derived via electron microscope, of the dance of a single atom.

In fact, National Geographic was becoming as familiar for its magnificent television programs, appearing four times a year, as for its yellow-bordered magazine. Blockbusters like The Incredible Machine (1975), The Sharks (1982), and Land of the Tiger (1985) were among the most watched shows ever televised on PBS. In 1985 National Geographic EXPLORER launched on cable television and featured episodes ranging

## MAPPING THE WORLD

Since the first one was published in the magazine in 1888, maps have been an integral component of many magazine articles, books, and television programs produced by the Society. Originally drafted by hand on large projections, today's maps are created by state-of-the art computers to chart everything from the Grand Canyon to the outer reaches of the universe.

**1979** Testaments to eternity and to the fragility of our resources, the stone sentinels of Easter Island mark a land where resources may have been completely exploited, forcing the ancient islanders to leave. Will such a fate befall Earth? In 1988 National Geographic sponsored programs and seminars as part of its Earth '88 symposium to find solutions to the Earth's problems.

from treks to Everest to poisonous snakes to war in Afghanistan.

In 1984 the Geographic added a fourth building to its campus. Dedicating it, President Ronald Reagan observed that the Society over the years had "brought home the profound truth that we are . . . a human family living together on a tiny blue-and-green planet." Nevertheless, Gil Grosvenor was worried. "Pick up a newspaper and every single day you'll see how geography plays a dominant role in giving a third dimension on life," he wrote. But test results showed that American schoolchildren knew little geography.

Grosvenor set out to change that. He began a geography education program, harnessing a national network of teacher training programs funded by a specially created foundation. A National Geographic Bee for grades four through

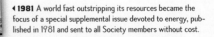

◀ **1981** A world fast outstripping its resources became the focus of a special supplemental issue devoted to energy, published in 1981 and sent to all Society members without cost.

◀ **1985** "You're nowhere unless you know where you are" became the mantra of Society President Gilbert M. Grosvenor, who undertook massive efforts to educate students about global relationships.

▲ **1981** Our precious planet seen from space

eight followed in 1989. And the Society helped compile geography learning standards for kindergarten through grade 12.

In 1988, the National Geographic Society celebrated its centennial. Its facilities were now unrivaled, the reach of its publications and programs now global. It had supported over 3,000 expeditions and research projects. Membership had passed ten million. At a star-studded black-tie dinner President-elect George H. W. Bush presided over a lavish celebration. Jacques Cousteau, Sir Edmund Hillary, Jane Goodall, Mary and Richard Leakey, and John Glenn were among the 15 explorers who received special Centennial Awards for their contributions to exploration and discovery. The prize was a crystal globe, symbol of our fragile Earth. ■

▼ **1988** Earth's "third Pole," Mount Everest, was mapped in painstaking detail for the December issue of *National Geographic* magazine.

# THE HEART
## OF ADVENTURE

*"Everyone is an explorer.
How could you possibly live
your life looking at a door
and not go open it?"*

**ROBERT BALLARD**

◄ **1999** Flying high over the Alps in the *Breitling Orbiter 3*, Bertrand Piccard and Brian Jones embark on the first nonstop circumnavigation of the globe by hot-air balloon. Almost 20 days and 29,018 miles later, on March 20, 1999, the two men achieved their goal.

**1989** Members of Will Steger's International Trans-Antarctica Expedition struggle through lunch.

**1999** For a decade following its 1999 debut, the award-winning National Geographic *Adventure* offered readers spine-tingling stories from the wilder edge.

▶ **1990** Deep in the murky waters of Siberia's Lake Baikal a joint Soviet-American team probes the abundant aquatic life of its unique ecosystem, which boasts more endemic species than any other lake. The 1990 expedition found that Baikal, the world's deepest lake, was once connected to the sea.

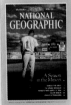

here is no better description of the spirit of modern adventure than that offered by Bertrand Piccard, who with Brian Jones in 1999 piloted *Breitling Orbiter 3* on the first nonstop hot-air balloon journey around the world. Writing in the September 1999 National Geographic, Piccard stated: "Human beings want to control nature, but to fly around the world by balloon, even using

◀ **1994** In April 1994 photographer William Albert Allard documented the heartbreak and the triumphs of "A Season in the Minors." Many of the photographs were later featured in a traveling exhibition.

our most advanced technology, we must harmonize with nature, following the rhythm of the wind."

Harmonizing with nature has increasingly come to define the Geographic's approach to exploration. Acknowledging this shift, President Gilbert M. Grosvenor, during the 1988 centennial celebrations, asserted that the Society had begun its first century "with a determination to better understand the world," but that it should commence its second by also encouraging "a better stewardship of the planet."

▲ **1995** Going out on a limb—or on a line— *National Geographic* photographers go to great lengths to gain new angles on the world.

To highlight the reality that the planet was still imperfectly understood, the Society in 1995 instituted an Explorers-in-Residence Program that has since been augmented by an annual class of emerging explorers as well. Will Steger, veteran leader of treks to both Poles, was first in a long line of very big names in exploration, each of whom would spend part of their time at headquarters and the remainder in the field. A glimpse of red feathers protruding from the ice led archaeologist Johan Reinhard, climbing high in the Peruvian Andes, to the mummy of a young Inca girl, dubbed the Ice Maiden. Study of her remains, over 500 years old, has led to valuable insights regarding ancient Inca sacrificial burial.

When Zahi Hawass headed Egypt's Supreme Council of Antiquities he communicated the excitement of archaeology to millions of National Geographic readers and viewers alike. "You never know what the sand will hide in the way of secrets," he once said. Paleontologist Paul Sereno had a pretty good idea, for he found in Saharan sands the remains of some of the largest carnivores ever to walk the Earth. The impressively named *Carcharodontosaurus saharicus* was perhaps larger than *Tyrannosaurus rex*, while the crocodile *Sarcosuchus imperator*—"SuperCroc"—was

▲ **1997** An expedition to Antarctica's remote Queen Maud Land is dwarfed by phantasmagoric peaks seldom seen by humans.

as long as a city bus and weighed ten tons. Both roamed Africa
when rivers coursed over what is now desert.

Other explorers-in-residence have included Meave Leakey,
director of the Koobi Fora camp on the shores of Kenya's Lake
Turkana, where a number of important hominid fossils have
been discovered. Her talented daughter, Louise, works closely
with her, and represents the third generation of the Leakey family
to work closely with the Geographic. Wade Davis, an ethnobota-
nist and student of indigenous cultures, has lived among tribal
peoples and is strongly committed to the preservation of their

ancient ways. Bob Ballard has not only located the wrecks of such World War II vessels as the *Bismarck, Yorktown,* and John F. Kennedy's PT-109, but has also found evidence of a cataclysmic flood in the prehistoric Black Sea. And in March 2012 Hollywood director James Cameron made the first solo dive to the Pacific's Challenger Deep, the first person to visit that deepest spot in the ocean since balloonist Bertrand Piccard's father, Jacques, did in 1960, alongside Don Walsh.

▲ **1995** Found high on an Andean peak, the "Ice Maiden" was sacrificed to the Inca gods about 500 years ago.

When President Gilbert M. Grosvenor retired in 1996 (and stepped down as Board Chairman in 2010), he left as his primary legacy a strong commitment to improving geography education at the primary and secondary school levels. Nevertheless, the family that had overseen the Society's growth and development since its founding now passed on the torch of leadership. Under Grosvenor's successors—especially John Fahey, Chief Executive Officer between 1998 and 2010 and now the Society's Chairman as well as CEO, and Tim Kelly, who is currently President—a venturesome new Geographic has been emerging, one that is striving to "inspire people to care about the planet."

NG *Traveler* magazine, for instance, has not only remained a leading publication in its field but also has taken the lead in promoting the sustainable-travel practices known as geotourism. It has even drawn up a Geotourism Charter to protect the geographic character of travel destinations—harmonizing

▲ **1998** Former head of Egypt's Supreme Council of Antiquities, Zahi Hawass was also a National Geographic explorer-in-residence. At left, a necklace ornament from a tomb in Abusir, near Cairo

**1993** A special extra issue of *National Geographic* published in 1993 addressed the planet's water crisis.

**2002** *National Geographic* has been increasingly tackling global health issues, including AIDS, overpopulation, and the war on disease.

with nature again—that emphasizes conservation values and encourages local community involvement. Though the pristine, unclimbed peaks of Antarctica's Queen Maud Land still retain what *Geographic* contributor Jon Krakauer described as "a bracing aura of terra incognita," they remain practically inaccessible to all but the most committed explorers. Yet aspiring geotourists who desire to see for themselves something of Antarctica can always turn to National Geographic Expeditions. Guided by seasoned explorers and other experts, they can trek high into the Himalaya, climb to the snows of Kilimanjaro, or visit remote villages in Papua New Guinea. Thanks to a partnership with Lindblad Expeditions, a pioneer in sustainable adventure travel, such geotourists can also cruise among the enchanted Galápagos Islands or along the edge of the polar ice packs.

# OLD BONES

## DIGGING FOR DINOSAURS

In 1907 National Geographic reported the discovery of "A Strange and Remarkable Beast"—a frozen mammoth recovered from the Siberian tundra. Since that moment paleontology—the study of life from past geologic periods—has captivated readers hungry for news of ancient beasts, especially dinosaurs. Roy Chapman Andrews thrilled readers with his discovery of the first intact nest of dinosaur eggs in Mongolia's harsh Gobi desert. Andrews reported the find in National Geographic, peppering his account with tales of dodging bandits. Some say Andrews was the real-life inspiration for Indiana Jones.

Paleontology made tremendous leaps in the 20th century, and the Society has supported a number of top researchers in the field, including Thomas Rich and Patricia Vickers-Rich, who shed light on "the dinosaurs of darkness," polar dinosaurs who inhabited Australia when it was still attached to Antarctica. Society grantees discovered the fossil of the world's largest lemur in Madagascar and remains of the world's oldest grasses, in present-day Nebraska and Kansas. Paul Sereno, an explorer-in-residence, has made spectacular finds, including "SuperCroc," a fossil the size of a city bus that is the most intact species of a giant crocodilian ever recovered. ∎

▲ **1925** Roy Chapman Andrews cradles a fossil dinosaur egg discovered in the Gobi desert.

◀ **1998** Skull of *Tyrannosaurus rex*

▼ **1990s** Workers uncover a prehistoric rhinoceros in present-day Nebraska.

Complementing such efforts to promote travel that harmonizes with the geographic character of places, the flagship National Geographic magazine has been reporting on a variety of issues with global implications. Especially under Editors Bill Allen (1995–2004) and Chris Johns (2005–present)—who took home the National Magazine Award for General Excellence, the industry's highest honor, three times during his first five years at the helm—the Geographic has been publishing stories on worldwide pandemics, the dark side of the diamond trade, and weapons of mass destruction alongside those announcing new archaeological discoveries or profiling scientific wonders. Articles on Somalia, malaria, nuclear waste, and Afghan women have been honored with prestigious accolades like the Overseas Press Club Award, while praise was heaped on single-topic issues concerning Africa or the growing scarcity of water resources. And as the magazine transitions to the digital

**▼ 1995** In 1995, *National Geographic* began publishing local-language editions. Today it is published in more than 30 languages each month.

**▶ 2004** Tearing across the prairie, a tornado sweeps up viewers on the increasingly popular National Geographic Channel. Storm chaser Tim Samaras, a National Geographic emerging explorer, races against such twisters to try to place instrument-laden probes squarely in their path.

era, subscribers to its iPad version have enjoyed such treats as a video of a sprinting cheetah shot with a Phantom high-definition digital camera.

Furthermore, the yellow-bordered journal has now been crossing other borders with dispatch. Since 1995, when the *Geographic* launched a Japanese-language edition, the magazine has gone truly international. Today more than 30 local-language editions—including Chinese, Korean, Arabic, Hebrew, and Bahasa Indonesian as well as those in nearly every tongue spoken from Spain to the Urals—are being printed each month. The impact has been astonishing. Today, one in four members reads *National Geographic* in a language other than English.

The success of the National Geographic Channel has had an even greater international impact. The

**2007** Always leader of the pack, Cesar Millan rehabilitates problem dogs and "trains" their owners. His Emmy-nominated *Dog Whisperer with Cesar Millan* has been a top-rated program on the National Geographic Channel since its 2004 debut.

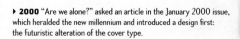

▶ **2000** "Are we alone?" asked an article in the January 2000 issue, which heralded the new millennium and introduced a design first: the futuristic alteration of the cover type.

▲ **1998** In the control room of his research vessel, Robert Ballard, discoverer of *Titanic*, *PT-109*, and other famous shipwrecks, carefully watches a video monitor. A National Geographic explorer-in-residence, Ballard has pioneered deep-sea exploration via remotely operated vehicles.

▶ **2005** *March of the Penguins*, a National Geographic co-production, won the 2005 Academy Award for best documentary.

National Geographic Channel debuted in 1997, initially in Europe and Australia, and soon became the fastest growing channel in the world. Two years after the January 2001 premiere of the domestic counterpart, it too was reaching more than 40 million homes. A decade later those numbers had skyrocketed.

While the Society's Television Specials and Explorer programs amassed even more Emmys (well over 100 today), the National Geographic Channels—for there are a multitude of them, including Nat Geo Wild, Nat Geo Adventure, and the Spanish-language network Nat Geo Mundo in addition to the original Channel—were the engines driving the Society's international growth, being beamed in 37 languages to some 435 million households in 173 countries.

Nevertheless, the Society has not confined itself to the small screen. It has also been producing feature films. In November 2000, while making *Frontline Diaries: Into the Forbidden Zone*, writer Sebastian Junger and photographer Reza were among the last Western journalists to interview legendary Afghan resistance leader Ahmad Shah Massoud. A decade later Junger was back in the Hindu Kush, embedded with a U.S. Army airborne unit engaged in combat operations against Taliban forces in a remote valley dubbed the "deadliest place on Earth." *Restrepo*, the Geographic-produced film he directed during this deployment, was nominated for a 2010 Academy Award.

Five years earlier the Society's *March of the Penguins* had actually won the coveted Oscar, honored for being that year's best documentary feature. The epic tale of the emperor penguins' urge to merge and the tribulations the birds were willing to undertake in order to raise chicks in the harshest

▲ **2002** National Geographic news, blogs, stories, maps, photographs, and a wealth of other resources are available with the click of a mouse at *nationalgeographic.com*. Launched in 1996, the site now attracts more than 20 million visitors a month.

◄ **1997** Inventor Mark W. Tilden shows off a few of his robotic creations: tiny insect robots that are powered by the sun. *National Geographic* caught up with the "Robot Revolution" in July 1997.

▶ **1991** Society grantee Nalini Nadkarni studies the unique ecosystems found in treetops. She climbs to her preferred perch via a "master caster," a rope-throwing gadget of her own devising.

## SMILE, YOU'RE ON CRITTERCAM

What would it be like to swim alongside a shark? The idea struck marine scientist Greg Marshall while diving in Belize. In 1987 he designed a prototype for the now famous Crittercam, a special video camera (seen below strapped to an emperor penguin) that has allowed scientists to study more than 25 marine species and view behavior never before observed. Marshall is now using Terrestrial Crittercam to aid in the study of land animals.

place on Earth attracted long lines of moviegoers to cinemas all over the world. A very different but no less moving saga, *God Grew Tired of Us*, premiered in 2006. It told the story of three Sudanese youths who, having fled the civil wars in their native land, overcame one adversity after another before being resettled in New York and Pittsburgh. The Society has been seeking out even larger screens. Its *Mysteries of Egypt* and *Lewis and Clark* broke records at large-format IMAX theaters. *Forces of Nature* and *Lions of the Kalahari* loomed gigantically out of the dark. Nor had there ever been a concert picture quite as spectacular as 2008's *U2 3D*, which was quite popular with viewers (wearing polarized glasses) in several countries. The Society was proud to distribute it, not only because it was the first live-action, digital 3-D film ever made but also because U2 was a band with planetary appeal that also possessed a

planetary perspective. It was a "band of the world" and, according to John Fahey, "world music is something the Geographic as an institution is really interested in."

It is interested in a number of other subjects, too, as even a cursory glance at the Society's website reveals. Nat Geo Music can indeed be found there, as can breaking news stories on new scientific discoveries; blogs contributed by far-flung

▲ **1996** After crossing 775 rugged miles of the Alaska Range, cyclists descend a thousand feet into Black Rock Glacier.

◄ **2008** National Geographic's *Green Guide*, available on *nationalgeographic.com*, features eco-friendly consumer choices.

# THE WAITING GAME

## NATURE PHOTOGRAPHY:
## A STANDARD OF EXCELLENCE

◢ **1999 Death drama on the African plains:** Chris Johns's photograph of cheetahs attacking a lechwe was published in December 1999. Though they run at speeds up to 65 miles an hour, cheetahs do not have the strength of larger cats. They held this lechwe underwater until it drowned, a behavior possibly never before captured on film.

"Wandering off into nature is not geography," grumbled one critical board member after a series of startling photographs made by pioneer wildlife photographer George Shiras were published in the July 1906 *National Geographic*. To most people today, however, wandering off into nature is what National Geographic does best.

Even before improved films, faster cameras, and telephoto lenses allowed more striking results, National Geographic photographers have been willing to wait patiently in blinds for hours upon hours, prey to flies and mosquitoes, sun and heat, rain and cold—to undergo almost any tribulation—to get just the right picture of birds on the wing or animals on the move.

As a result, every kind of nature photography has found expression somewhere at the Geographic, whether in the pages of the magazines or books or in the television documentaries that have won for the Society's Natural History Film Division more than 30 Emmys and every major award for wildlife films. Whether it's the changing world of an apple tree or curious pictures of bizarre insects and strange wildflowers or the immemorial drama of predator and prey on the shimmering African plains, whether it is the stunning glory of reef and fish or the graceful arc of a breaching whale or the

dangerous proximity of the shark, nature photography has come to play a fundamental role in the Geographic's presentation of the world. ■

correspondents and photographers; information on environmental issues; a *Green Guide* promoting more sustainable living (while also explaining how the Geographic's own headquarters recycles trash and conserves energy); teaching resources; weird and wacky facts; cool clicks for kids; and of course maps, photos, video clips, and a ubiquitous button: Learn More. Upwards of 20 million people a month visit this online bazaar of information. When combined with the Society's television efforts, feature films, National Geographic circulation, the durably popular NG Kids and NG Little Kids magazines, and an array of exhibitions and live events, that number swells twentyfold: The Society now reaches hundreds of millions of people a month, around the clock as around the globe. No wonder Fahey once commented, "National

Geographic is an incredible mix of science and education, of media and mission, of storytellers and explorers, all working to inspire people to care about the planet."

It can be grueling work, though. On September 20, 1999, Explorer-in-Residence Michael Fay stepped off into the bush of the Republic of the Congo. For the next 15 months the wildlife biologist crossed more than 2,000 miles of pristine central African rain forest—on foot, wearing sandals, following a line straight through seemingly impenetrable forest. Battling leeches, scorpions, parasites, and driving rain, plunging through swamps, dodging vipers and deadly Ebola virus, encountering animals that had never before seen a human being, Fay amassed an unprecedented amount of information about a still remarkably unspoiled wilderness. Through Internet installments and three

▲ **1989** A lone baobab tree in the Australian outback.

▼ **2003** Gabon's conserved land is marked on the map below.

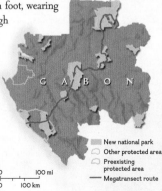

GABON

0        100 mi
0      100 km

New national park
Other protected area
Preexisting protected area
Megatransect route

National Geographic articles, Fay's Megatransect transfixed the imagination of millions. Staff photographer Michael "Nick" Nichols's spellbinding photographs captured the primordial enchantment of this "green abyss" and helped persuade the government of Gabon to set aside 10 percent of its national territory—forests that might otherwise have gone to timber companies—to create 13 national parks. Meanwhile, his fellow explorers-in-residence have been matching his achievements by helping preserve those "rain forests of the sea," coral reefs. In 2006, for instance, Sylvia Earle had helped persuade President George W. Bush to establish what is now called the Papahānaumokuākea Marine National Monument, nearly 140,000 square miles of ocean, coral, and island stretching northwest of Oahu and Hawaii—a reserve larger than all the U.S. national parks (outside Alaska) combined. Soon afterward,

Enric Sala—who, while growing up in Spain, had been inspired to become a marine ecologist by watching Jacques Cousteau on television—launched the Society's Pristine Seas Initiative, an effort to locate and inventory the few coral reefs that remain healthy ecosystems. So far his efforts have resulted in Chile establishing a 58,000-square-mile marine park about the island of Salas y Gómez, and Costa Rica creating a reserve almost as large around Cocos Island.

Such achievements echo that "better stewardship of the planet" to which the Society is pledged. Indeed, John Fahey has reiterated that "conservation is a key component of our mission in the 21st century." It's a fair guess, then, that in the coming years most of the explorers who will be associated with the National Geographic will be concerned with ecological issues such as dwindling resources, overpopulation, and the looming extinction of cultural and biological diversity.

◀ **2007** Marine predators, like gray reef sharks and red snappers hovering over the Pacific Ocean's Kingman Reef, indicate healthy coral reef ecosystems.

▲ **2011** Gerlinde Kaltenbrunner is the first woman to summit all 14 of the world's 8,000-meter peaks without using supplementary oxygen.

When in 2011 Krithi Karanth received Society funding to examine human-wildlife interactions in India, it was the 10,000th research grant the Geographic has awarded in the century and a quarter of its existence. Daughter of one of the Indian subcontinent's most prominent wildlife biologists, Karanth represents a new generation of explorers that, in her words, feels the responsibility to "act now using the best science and link it to constructive, on-ground conservation action."

Even geneticists like Spencer Wells sense that they are racing against time. Explorer-in-Residence Wells heads up the Society's Genographic Project, leading an international team of researchers that analyzes historical patterns in DNA being contributed by hundreds of thousands of people worldwide. The results allow Wells to chart the greatest journey in human history, one that commenced some 60,000 years ago when a small band of Homo sapiens began trekking out of Africa, for their descendants were destined to populate the world.

Yet globalization, by intermixing today's populations on an unprecedented scale, is scrambling the genetic sequences Wells is collecting from once isolated indigenous peoples, obscuring the story of our origins. It is also eroding thousands of culturally distinct

## DIGITAL EXPLOSION

One swipe of your mobile, and the world of National Geographic is literally at hand. Fully downloadable editions of both *NG Traveler* and *National Geographic* are at your fingertips, as are an interactive globe and an atlas app (that when released in 2010 was downloaded more than one million times), as well as video clips, news bites, interviews, blogs, and games, all available on a variety of mobile platforms. Oh, and plenty of photos, too.

iPad is a trademark of Apple Inc., registered in the U.S. and other countries.

expressions of our common humanity, and to linguist K. David Harrison, lost languages are as irreplaceable as lost species. That's why Harrison launched the Society's Enduring Voices Project: to help preserve the world's remaining stock of linguistic diversity.

Digital expeditions represent another new frontier in exploration. Albert Lin, for example, hopes to solve a long-standing mystery— the whereabouts of Genghis Khan's tomb—without turning a spadeful of dirt. He is instead perusing satellite imagery of Mongolia, and turning to the World Wide Web for help. Hundreds of volunteers have analyzed thousands of images, geo-tagging landscape features that might be promising clues. This unique "crowd sourcing" approach even prompted the United Nations Refugee Agency to approach Emerging Explorer Patrick Meier, seeking to mount a similar geo-tagging of satellite imagery to better estimate the number of refugees fleeing violence in Somalia. "Digital expeditions like these can democratize the next frontier of exploration," Meier says.

Whether it be people donating DNA to the Genographic Project or geo-tagging satellite images of Mongolia from their living room or joining forces with wildlife filmmakers Dereck and Beverly Joubert—who, alarmed at the precipitous fall in the numbers of lions, tigers, leopards, snow leopards, and jaguars established the Society's Big Cats Initiative, reaching out through the Internet and urging people everywhere to

▼ **2012** James Cameron's *DEEPSEA CHALLENGER* undergoes a test dive.

▼ **2011** An NGS film clip of a honey badger eating anything it encounters, including a viper, went viral when a comic version was uploaded to YouTube.

▲ **2006** A speaker of Murrinh-Patha, one of Australia's indigenous languages, relates a Dreaming story.

▶ **2009** A colossal face coalesces from a pillar of gas and dust in the Carina Nebula.

"cause an uproar"—there is a growing consensus, faced with the challenges we confront today, that we can accomplish more together than we can individually.

Banding together to achieve a greater good—"the increase and diffusion of geographical knowledge"—is, after all, what drew those 33 founders to the Cosmos Club that foggy night in January 1888. "In union there is strength," Gardiner Greene Hubbard announced to the Society's 165 members later that same month, "and through the medium of a national organization, we may hope to promote geographic research in a manner that could not be accomplished by scattered individuals, or by local

◀ **2008** A special issue devoted entirely to one country, the May 2008 *National Geographic* explores the "terrain of exuberance and anxiety that is China today."

societies . . ." Today that Society has become an international organization embracing a planetary perspective, and over the course of the past 125 years its leaders have so broadened its mission that former President Jimmy Carter, for one, could declare that the National Geographic had done more than any other organization that he knew "to tie the people of different nations together, and to let us know and understand one another." Though the world may now be charted, its Poles attained, its highest mountains climbed, that same need to join together to better understand it—its peoples and nations, animals and plants, its deepest seas, fiery core, and place among the twirling galaxies—is more crucial than ever. ■

▲ **1995** Chris Johns gets a bird's-eye view of East Africa's Rift Valley.

▼ **2011** *Angry Birds* features 50 angry avians, plus characters from the game.

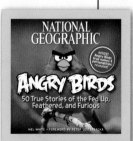

# NATIONAL GEOGRAPHIC SOCIETY

## GRANTS & EXPEDITIONS

• National Geographic research grant

miles 3,000

kilometers 5,000

National Geographic explorers and scientists have circled the globe thousands of times in the pursuit of geographic knowledge. This map reflects the field locations of National Geographic grants and expeditions since 1970. The red markers represent less than half of the 10,000 grants awarded in the history of the Society.

# THE HUBBARD MEDAL

**N**amed for a Society founder and awarded for distinction in exploration, discovery, and research, the Hubbard Medal has been awarded to 75 of the world's most intrepid explorers. President Theodore Roosevelt presented the Hubbard to its first recipient, Robert E. Peary, in 1906. On the Arctic map that adorned the back of the medal a blue sapphire star marked the "farthest north" point Peary had achieved. In 2000 the Hubbard was awarded posthumously to Peary's companion, Matthew Alexander Henson. Henson's granddaughter, a Society employee, accepted the medal in his name.

**2012**  Jacques Piccard
For contributions to exploration through being a member of the first team to dive to the bottom of the Mariana Trench in 1960

**2011**  Gilbert M. Grosvenor
For distinction in exploration, discovery, and research

**2010**  Don Walsh
For contributions to exploration through being a member of the first team to dive to the bottom of the Mariana Trench in 1960

**2000**  Matthew Alexander Henson
For being one of the first of two to reach the North Pole

**1999**  Brian Jones and Bertrand Piccard
For Breitling Orbiter 3 around-the-world balloon record

**1996**  Robert D. Ballard
For extraordinary accomplishments in undersea exploration

**1995**  Jane Goodall
For her extraordinary study of wild chimpanzees

**1994**  Richard Leakey
For protecting the Earth's wildlife and illuminating the origins of humanity

**1994**  Gilbert F. White
For unwavering dedication to geography, environmental science, and education

**1981**  Robert L. Crippen and John W. Young
For contributions to space science as crew of the space shuttle Columbia

**1978**  Bruce Charles Heezen and Marie Tharp
For contributions to knowledge of the ocean floor

**1978**  James E. Webb
For outstanding contribution to manned lunar landings

**1975**  Alexander Wetmore
For contributions to ornithology

**1970**  Edwin A. Aldrin, Neil A. Armstrong, and Michael Collins
For space exploration; first moon landing as the crew of Apollo 11

**1969**    William A. Anders, Frank Borman, and James A. Lovell
For space exploration; first to orbit the moon as crew of Apollo 8

**1967**    Juan T. Trippe
For contributions to aviation

**1963**    American Mount Everest Expedition
For contributions to geography through conquest of Earth's highest mountain

**1962**    John H. Glenn, Jr.
For space exploration

**1962**    Dr. Louis S. B. Leakey and Mrs. Louis S. B. Leakey
For anthropological discoveries in East Africa

**1959**    Sir Vivian Fuchs
For leadership of British trans-Antarctic expedition

**1959**    U.S. Navy Antarctic Expeditions
For Antarctic research and exploration 1955–1959

**1958**    Paul A. Siple
For 30 years of Antarctic explorations, including leadership of first group
to winter at the South Pole

**1954**    British Everest Expedition
For first ascent of Mount Everest

**1953**    Cmdr. Donald B. MacMillan
For Arctic explorations 1908–1952

**1945**    Henry H. Arnold
For contributions to aviation

**1936**    Lincoln Ellsworth
For extraordinary achievements in polar exploration

**1935**    Orvil A. Anderson and Albert W. Stevens
For world altitude record of 72,395 feet in balloon Explorer II

**1934**    Anne Morrow Lindbergh
For notable flights as co-pilot on Charles Lindbergh's aerial surveys

**1931**    Roy Chapman Andrews
For geographic discoveries in Central Asia

**1930**    Richard E. Byrd, Jr.
Special Medal of Honor: First to attain the South Pole by air.

**1927**    Charles A. Lindbergh
For New York–Paris solo flight

**1926**    Richard E. Byrd, Jr.
For being first to reach North Pole by airplane

**1919**    Vilhjamur Stefansson
For discoveries in the Canadian Arctic

**1910**    Ernest H. Shackleton
For Antarctic explorations and farthest south

**1909**    Robert A. Bartlett
For far-north explorations with Peary's 1909 expedition

**1909**    Grove Karl Gilbert
For 30 years of achievements in physical geography

**1909**    Robert E. Peary
Special Medal of Honor: Discovery of the North Pole

**1907**    Roald Amundsen
For traverse of Northwest Passage

**1906**    Robert E. Peary
For Arctic explorations

# INDEX

Boldface indicates illustrations.

# ILLUSTRATIONS CREDITS

Cover: Wallis W. Nutting.

Title Page: Gordon Wiltsie.

Contents Page: Volkmar Wentzel.

Introduction: 6, Mark Thiessen, NGS; 7, Mike Hennig.

Chapter 1: 1888–1920
8, NGS Image Collection; 10, Stanley Meltzoff; 11 (UP), Peter Bissett; 11 (LO), NGS Archives; 12 (UP), William Henry Holmes; 12 (LO), Greely Papers, Library of Congress; 13 (UP), NGS Archives/Mark Thiessen, NGS; 13 (LO), from *Tent Life in Siberia*, G.P. Putnam & Sons, 1910; 14, Robert E. Peary Collection, NGS; 16-17, Eliza R. Scidmore; 18 (UP), John K. Hillers, National Anthropological Archives, Smithsonian Institution; 18 (LO), NGS Archives; 19 (UP), NGS Archives; 19 (LO), Harris & Ewing; 20 (UP), I.C. Russell Collection, U.S. Geological Survey; 20 (LO), NGS Archives/Mark Thiessen, NGS; 21 (UP), NGS Archives; 21 (LO), Asst. Paymaster J.Q. Lovell, USN; 22 (UP), Alexander Graham Bell Collection; 22 (LO), Grosvenor Collection, NGS; 23 (UP), Grosvenor Collection, NGS; 23 (LO), NGS Archives/Robin Siegel; 24 (UP), Courtesy DC Public Library, Washingtoniana Division; 24 (LO), Eliza R. Scidmore; 25 (UP), John Alexander Douglas McCurdy; 25 (LO), NGS Archives; 26 (UP), Donald B. Mac-Millan; 28 (UP), George F. Mobley; 29 (UP), Robert F. Benson; 29 (LO), NGS Archives; 30, Edward S. Curtis; 30-31, NGS Archives; 31, George Shiras, III; 32 (UP), Hiram Bingham; 32 (LO), NGS Archives; 33 (UP), Lawrence Martin; 33 (LO), NGS Archives; 34 (UP), NGS Archives/Rebecca Hale, NGS; 34 (LO), Robert Caputo; 35 (UP), Christina Krysto; 35 (LO), NGS Archives.

Chapter 2: 1921–1956
36, Joseph F. Rock 38-39, American Colony Photographers; 40 (UP), B. Anthony Stewart; 40 (LO), NGS Archives; 41 (UP), Underwood & Underwood/CORBIS; 41 (LO), William Wisner Chapin; 42, Franklin Price Knott; 43 (UP), Oscar D. Von Engeln; 43 (LO), NGS Archives/Mark Thiessen, NGS; 44 (UP), Charles Martin; 44 (LO), W.H. Longley and Charles Martin; 45 (UP), Maynard Owen Williams; 45 (LO), NGS Archives; 46 (LE, BOTH), NGS Archives; 46 (RT), Howell Walker; 47 (UP), Maynard Owen Williams; 47 (LO), NGS Archives; 48 (UP), W. Robert Moore;

48 (LO), N.C. Wyeth; 49 (UP), White House collection, photo by Joseph D. Lavenburg; 49 (LO), B. Anthony Stewart; 50 (UP), © Harold Edgerton, 2012, courtesy of Palm Press, Inc.; 50 (LO), David Knudsen; 51 (UP), Tom Lovell; 51 (LO), Major H. Lee Wells, Jr.; 52 (LE), Richard H. Stewart; 52 (RT), Charles Martin; 53 (UP LE), Albert Moldvay; 53 (UP RT), James L. Stanfield; 53 (LO), NGS Archives/Robin Siegel; 54, Luis Marden; 55 (BOTH), Luis Marden; 56 (UP LE), NGS Archives; 56 (UP RT), Thomas Nebbia; 56 (LO), NGS Archives; 57 (UP), Howell Walker; 57 (LO), NGS Archives.

Chapter 3: 1957–1969
58, Wilbur E. Garrett; 60-61, Hugo van Lawick; 62 (UP), Barry Bishop; 62 (LO), NGS Archives; 63 (UP), NGS Archives/Robin Siegel; 63 (LO), NGS Archives; 64 (UP), Thomas J. Abercrombie; 64 (LO, BOTH), NGS Archives; 65 (UP), Thomas J. Abercrombie; 65 (LO), Robert B. Goodman; 66 (UP), Robert F. Sisson; 66 (LO), Jane Goodall; 67, NGS Archives/Robin Siegel; 68 (LE), Gilbert H. Grosvenor; 68 (RT), Ray V. Davis; 69 (UP), Frank and John Craighead; 69 (LO), NGS Archives; 70 (UP), NG Maps; 70 (LO), Dean Conger for NASA; 71 (UP), Edwin L. Wisherd; 71 (LO), William Taub, NASA; 72 (UP), Vincent Di Fate; 72 (LO LE), Charlie Archambault; 72 (LO RT), Robert F. Sisson; 73 (BOTH), Wilbur E. Garrett; 74, Samuel C. Silverstein; 75 (UP), Bradford Washburn; 75 (LO, BOTH), NGS Archives/Robin Siegel; 76 (UP), W.L. Newton III; 76 (LO), NGS Archives; 77 (UP), Charles Allmon; 77 (LO), W. Robert Moore.

Chapter 4: 1970–1987
78, Dian Fossey; 80-81, Steve Raymer; 82 (UP), Dewitt Jones; 82 (LO), NGS Archives; 83 (UP), James P. Blair; 83 (LO), Rebecca Hale, NGS; 84 (UP), Jodi Cobb; 84 (LO), James P. Blair; 85 (UP), NGS Archives; 85 (LO), Leroy Woodson; 86 (UP), Emory Kristof; 86 (LO LE), NGS Archives; 86 (LO RT), George B. Schaller; 87 (UP), Bianca Lavies; 87 (LO), Luis Marden; 88 (BOTH), Mark Thiessen, NGS; 89 (UP), James L. Stanfield; 89 (LO), NGS Archives; 90 (UP LE), NGS Archives; 90 (UP RT), AP Photo/J. Scott Applewhite; 90 (LO), NGS Archives; 91 (UP), Dean Conger; 91 (LO), James L. Stanfield; 92 (UP LE), Bruce Dale; 92 (UP RT), Emory Kristof; 92 (LO), Bill Ballenberg; 93 (BOTH), O. Louis Mazzatenta; 94, David Doubilet; 95 (UP), NGS Archives; 95 (CTR), Robert S. Oakes; 95 (LO), Al Giddings Images; 96 (UP LE), NGS Archives; 96 (UP RT), Dr. Barry Filshie and

Colin Beaton; 96 (LO), Lloyd K. Townsend and Ellen Kuzdro; 97 (UP), Jonathan Blair; 97 (LO), B. Anthony Stewart; 98 (UP), Gordon Gahan; 98 (LO), NGS Archives; 99 (UP LE), Marie-Louise Brimberg; 99 (UP RT), NASA; 99 (LO), NG Maps.

Chapter 5: 1988–Present
100, AP Photo/Keystone/Fabrice Coffrini; 102-103, Will Steger; 104 (UP LE), NGS Archives; 104 (UP RT), Bill Curtsinger; 104 (LO), NGS Archives; 105 (LO), Bobby Model/National Geographic Stock; 105 (LO), Gordon Wiltsie; 106, Mark Read; 107 (UP), Stephen L. Alvarez; 107 (CTR), Kenneth Garrett; 107 (LO), Kenneth Garrett; 108 (UP), Jim Richardson; 108 (LO), NGS Archives; 109 (UP), James B. Shackelford, American Museum of Natural History #410764; 109 (CTR), Ira Block; 109 (LO), Annie Griffiths; 110 (LE, BOTH), NGS Archives; 110 (RT), Carsten Peter; 111 (UP), Evan Hurd; 111 (LO), NGS Archives; 112 (UP), David Doubilet; 112 (LO), NGS Archives; 113 (UP), courtesy NG On-Line; 113 (LO), George Steinmetz; 114 (UP), Mark W. Moffett; 114 (LO), Greg Marshall, NGS; 115 (UP), Bill Hatcher; 115 (LO), NGS Archives; 116, Chris Johns, NGS; 117 (UP), David Doubilet; 117 (LO LE), George Grall; 117 (LO RT), Bianca Lavies; 118 (UP), Michael Nichols, NGS; 118 (LO LE), NGS Archives/Mark Thiessen, NGS; 118 (LO RT), Michael Nichols, NGS; 119 (UP), Sam Abell; 119 (LO), NG Maps; 120 (LE), Mark Thiessen, NGS; 120 (RT), Grizzly Creek Films, LLC; 121 (UP), NGS Archives; 121 (LO), Brian Skerry; 122 (UP), Tommy Heinrich; 122 (LO), NGM on iPad; iPad is a trademark of Apple Inc., registered in the U.S. and other countries; 123 (UP), Mark Thiessen, NGS; 123 (LO), Meoita/Shutterstock; 124 (UP LE), Chris Rainier/National Geographic Enduring Voices Project; 124 (UP RT), NASA, ESA, and the Hubble SM4 ERO Team; 124 (LO), NGS Archives; 125 (UP), Kent Kobersteen; 125 (LO), used with permission of Rovio.

Grants & Expeditions: 126-127, NG Maps; 127 (flag), Martin Rogers.

Hubbard Medal: Robert S. Oakes.

Back Cover: Robert E. Peary Collection, NGS (Peary portrait); Emory Kristof (Titanic); Kent Kobersteen (Chris Johns at volcano); Steve McCurry (portrait on cover of June 1985 *National Geographic* magazine).

## ON ASSIGNMENT WITH

# NATIONAL GEOGRAPHIC

Mark Collins Jenkins

CELEBRATING
‹125›
YEARS

### PUBLISHED BY THE NATIONAL GEOGRAPHIC SOCIETY

John M. Fahey, Chairman of the Board and Chief Executive Officer

Timothy T. Kelly, President

Declan Moore, Executive Vice President; President, Publishing and Digital Media

Melina Gerosa Bellows, Executive Vice President; Chief Creative Officer, Books, Kids, and Family

### PREPARED BY THE BOOK DIVISION

Hector Sierra, Senior Vice President and General Manager

Jonathan Halling, Design Director, Books and Children's Publishing

Marianne R. Koszorus, Design Director, Books

Lisa Thomas, Senior Editor

R. Gary Colbert, Production Director

Jennifer A. Thornton, Director of Managing Editorial

Susan S. Blair, Director of Photography

Meredith C. Wilcox, Director, Administration and Rights Clearance

### STAFF FOR THIS BOOK

Renee Braden, Project Editor

Melissa Farris, Peggy Archambault, Art Directors

Cathy Hunter, Researcher and Contributing Writer

Carl Mehler, Director of Maps

Priit Vesilind, Joe Blanton, Contributing Writers

Marshall Kiker, Michael O'Connor, Associate Managing Editors

Judith Klein, Production Editor

Lisa A. Walker, Production Manager

Galen Young, Rights Clearance Specialist

Katie Olsen, Production Design Assistant

### MANUFACTURING AND QUALITY MANAGEMENT

Phillip L. Schlosser, Senior Vice President

Chris Brown, Vice President, NG Book Manufacturing

George Bounelis, Vice President, Production Services

Nicole Elliott, Manager

Rachel Faulise, Manager

Robert L. Barr, Manager

The National Geographic Society is one of the world's largest nonprofit scientific and educational organizations. Founded in 1888 to "increase and diffuse geographic knowledge," the Society's mission is to inspire people to care about the planet. It reaches more than 400 million people worldwide each month through its official journal, National Geographic, and other magazines; National Geographic Channel; television documentaries; music; radio; films; books; DVDs; maps; exhibitions; live events; school publishing programs; interactive media; and merchandise. National Geographic has funded more than 10,000 scientific research, conservation and exploration projects and supports an education program promoting geographic literacy. For more information, visit www .nationalgeographic.com.

For more information, please call 1-800-NGS LINE (647-5463) or write to the following address:

National Geographic Society
1145 17th Street N.W.
Washington, D.C. 20036-4688 U.S.A.

For information about special discounts for bulk purchases, please contact National Geographic Books Special Sales: ngspecsales@ngs.org

For rights or permissions inquiries, please contact National Geographic Books Subsidiary Rights: ngbookrights@ngs.org

ISBN: 978-1-4262-1013-6

Printed in the United States of America
12/WOR/1

# Join the Adventure!

To order National Geographic magazine, National Geographic Traveler, and National Geographic Kids, call: 1-800 NGS LINE (800 647 5463) or 800 548 9797 (TDD) or visit nationalgeographic.com/magazines

For special interactive features and more information about the National Geographic Society's programs, books, videos, gift catalog, expeditions, photography, and maps visit nationalgeographic.com

Visit channel.nationalgeographic.com/ (U.S.) or nationalgeographic.com/siteindex/international to find out what's on—and how to get the Channel in your area.

Explorers Hall is the National Geographic Society's museum space located at Society headquarters in Washington, D.C. For directions, hours, and exhibition schedules visit nationalgeographic.com/explorer

To order additional copies of this book, call 1-888-647-6733

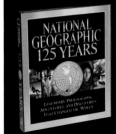